bigcat diary Cheetah

big Cat diary Cheetah

Jonathan and Angela Scott

Collins

To Cissy and David Walker, who have been the most generous of friends and tireless supporters of Friends of Conservation.

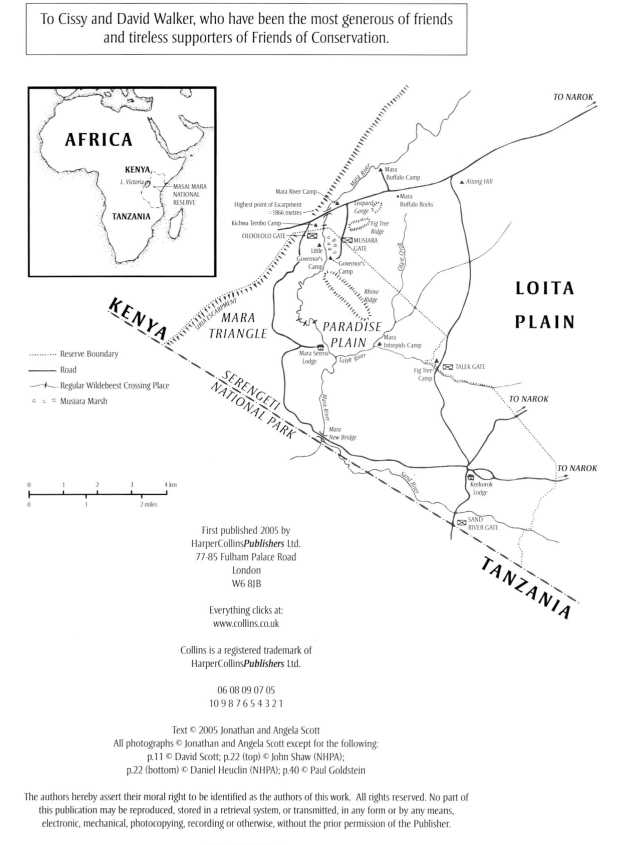

Reserve Boundary

Road

Regular Wildebeest Crossing Place

Musiara Marsh

0 1 2 3 4 km

0 1 2 miles

First published 2005 by
HarperCollins*Publishers* Ltd.
77-85 Fulham Palace Road
London
W6 8JB

Everything clicks at:
www.collins.co.uk

Collins is a registered trademark of
HarperCollins*Publishers* Ltd.

06 08 09 07 05
10 9 8 7 6 5 4 3 2 1

Text © 2005 Jonathan and Angela Scott
All photographs © Jonathan and Angela Scott except for the following:
p.11 © David Scott; p.22 (top) © John Shaw (NHPA);
p.22 (bottom) © Daniel Heuclin (NHPA); p.40 © Paul Goldstein

ISBN 0 00 7149204

Edited by Caroline Taggart
Designed by Liz Sephton

Colour reproduction by Colourscan, Singapore
Printed and bound in Singapore

Contents

Introduction

Each book in this collection of three titles on Africa's big cats has been written both as a companion to the television series *Big Cat Diary* and as an opportunity to explore the latest research on lions, leopards and cheetahs throughout the continent, using our work in the Masai Mara National Reserve in Kenya to help illustrate the various topics. My greatest concern was that by the time we started work on *Cheetah*, the programme might have vanished from our screens. Seven years is a long time in television, and we have held our breath on five occasions now, wondering if *BCD* would be recommissioned. The fact that the latest series was moved from its comfortable Sunday afternoon slot on BBC2 – family hour on this factual/special-interest channel – to prime time on BBC1 says much for the way the series has evolved. *Big Cat Diary* has always been perceived as excellent wildlife viewing – and who could argue with that, given the kind of footage the cameramen have produced over the years, with car-climbing cheetahs, lions desperately defending young cubs against buffaloes or wrestling a hippo to the ground, and a leopard who captured the hearts of audiences the world over as she struggled to raise her cubs? But now the programme is also seen as 'good entertainment' – the litmus test of what does or does not appear on mainstream television.

The BBC's recent decision to axe the long-running *Wildlife on One* – a series of half-hour programmes each dedicated to the behaviour of a particular species – is symptomatic of the current attitude to wildlife on television. Audiences' tastes have changed and, for the moment at least, wildlife documentaries, rich on behaviour and beautifully shot over the course of many months – years even – are too expensive, and in many cases not entertaining enough, to justify their airtime. The big blue-chip productions pioneered by David Attenborough, such as *Life on Earth* and more recently Alistair Fothergill's *Blue Planet*, still make compelling viewing. But they cost millions of pounds, and only something like the BBC Natural History Unit, with the help of co-production money from the Discovery

View from Rhino Ridge overlooking Paradise Plain. The broad spectrum of habitats the Mara offers to both predators and prey is the reason it supports such varied and prolific wildlife.

Grey crowned cranes, Musiara Marsh. Cranes perform an elegant nuptial dance during the breeding season, and have a beautiful mournful call.

Young female defassa waterbuck. These large, long-haired antelopes favour areas of lush vegetation, where adults are sometimes taken by lions, and calves by leopards.

I have been fortunate in that the new wave favours presenters as a means of communicating immediacy to what is happening – and to fill time in a cost-effective way. But there has also been a tendency to dumb-down the product or to rely on old footage, making some programmes short on meaningful content. In many cases, the more extreme the programme, the more entertaining it is perceived to be; so wrestling with crocodiles and messing with dangerous snakes have become hugely popular. People love action and a sense of danger, though I am not sure that this approach has done much either for the animals or for conservation, simply perpetuating the old adage of nature red in tooth and claw, with a buffalo lurking around every corner ready to flatten some unsuspecting human. In fact, most animals do everything possible to avoid contact with humans.

Meanwhile, *Big Cat Diary* has endured because of audiences' fascination with the beauty and power of its subjects, and the enthusiasm that the presenters generate from being able to spend long periods with these intriguing creatures. There has been no need to resort to hype to make the big cats interesting or exciting – their lives are by their very nature full of drama. Even so, when the fifth series of *BCD* was moved to a prime-time slot, none of us was prepared for the response it generated.

To be considered a success, wildlife programmes airing at 7 p.m. on the mainstream channel are expected to draw a minimum audience of 4 million. We were painfully aware of what had happened when *BCD* was launched on BBC1 in 1996 and we found ourselves airing at the same time as Manchester United in the European Cup. On that occasion we pulled in 2 million viewers – quite respectable under the circumstances. The next three series, shown on BBC2, drew upwards of 3 million and scored top marks for viewer satisfaction. But television is always eager to try something new, so it was decided to

Channel (or its wildlife strand Animal Planet) can afford to make them. The latest of such programmes, *Planet Earth*, will be five years in the making at a cost of around £16 million. With the use of innovative technology to provide viewers with a new vision of our planet's wildlife, a worldwide audience is virtually guaranteed – and it will be money well spent. But for the smaller independent production companies, finding funding is no easy matter, regardless of how original their ideas are.

package this fifth series as an 'event' and to call it *Big Cat Week*, with five 30-minute-programmes shown on consecutive nights, Monday to Friday, preceded by a media blitz. This time round everybody knew about *Big Cat Diary*, and the fact that audience figures climbed steadily throughout the week meant that people were talking about it. Monday's programme drew 5.6 million viewers, Friday's over 7 million, making it the most popular wildlife series since *Blue Planet* three years earlier.

Big Cat Week had all the excitement of live television but, with the luxury of more time for filming than is possible in a genuinely live broadcast, there was no risk that the wildebeest might not show up or that the lions would do very little other than find a shady spot to rest during the day. Nor were we anchored to a small radius of operation because we had to be within line of sight of the receiver, as had been the case when Julian Pettifer and I presented a series of live programmes from the Mara called *Africa Watch* in 1989. But there were time constraints nonetheless. Earlier series of *BCD*, consisting first of six and later of eight half-hour programmes, had been filmed over the course of ten weeks. For *Big Cat Week* we were given just one month. This was pushing things to the limit. Four editors worked flat out at our base camp in the Mara to cut sequences and make sure that all the presenter-led material had been shot before the final day of filming, using as little voice-over as possible to maintain the sense of presenters 'being there'. The editors then finished compiling the programmes back at the Natural History Unit in Bristol. Somehow the Mara had worked its magic yet again.

Writing about cheetahs was always going to be the most challenging aspect of the *BCD* books, simply because over the years Angie and I had spent so much of our time in the Mara watching lions or searching for leopards. Like most first-time visitors to Africa, I was mesmerized by the lion and intrigued by the leopard – and I had only to hear that a pack of wild dogs had been sighted to set off in pursuit of them, regardless of how far I had to travel. The sheer physical presence of a lion strikes a chord deep within all of us – those golden eyes, tawny hide and regal bearing cast an irresistible spell. They are warrior kings, and their group-based way of life marks them out among the other cats – they are at once endearingly social and consummate killers. Seeing a pride of lions moving confidently through the long red-oat grass to the place they have chosen to rest is an everyday occurrence for visitors to the Mara. I simply cannot imagine a game drive here without seeing lions – there are more than 500 of them in the Mara's 1510km² (583sq. miles), perhaps five times the number of leopards and ten times the number of cheetahs. And the fact that you are far more likely to spot a cheetah than a leopard on an early-morning game drive just heightens the appeal of my favourite African animal.

I simply took the cheetahs for granted. They were so visible, striding out across the rolling plains or resting in the shade of a solitary boscia tree, and they lacked that extra element of controlled menace that made their more powerful cousins so fascinating. I wrote about them in some of my early books, though only in passing. But when Angie and I did go in search of cheetahs – something we made a point of doing when we were collecting material for our book *The Big Cat Diary* (co-authored with our good friend Brian Jackman) in 1996 – we loved every moment spent in the company of these graceful felines. Who could fail to marvel at the cheetah's breathtaking burst of speed as it chased after its prey? Now we felt exhilarated by the possibility of getting to know cheetahs as intimately as the lions and leopards who make a safari to the Masai Mara such a memorable experience.

For the first three series of *BCD*, my co-presenter Simon King narrated the cheetah story, I followed the leopards and we

Fifty per cent of prides in the Mara are accompanied by two adult males. It would be impossible for a single male to defend a territory for long here, where there is one of the highest densities of lions in Africa.

Angie is the production stills photographer for *Big Cat Diary* and helps to find the big cats for our film crews. We use a range of lenses from 15mm to 600mm.

shared the lions. That made sense. I had written about the leopards I had got to know since the 1970s, Simon had filmed cheetahs in the Mara in the 1990s and with his partner Marguerite Smits van Oyen was working on a television special for the BBC's *Natural World* series, based on their attempts to release two male cheetah cubs in the Lewa Downs Wildlife Conservancy in the beautifully rugged Laikipia District in northern Kenya. In addition, we had both either filmed or written about the Marsh Lions – the same pride that I had followed for the past 27 years – and knew many of the cats as individuals. That ensured that we could communicate our love of the area and our passion for Africa's big cats to our audience.

We were joined for the fourth series by Saba Douglas-Hamilton, whose parents Iain and Oria had pioneered elephant research in Tanzania in the 1960s, and who, like Angie, had been born and brought up in Africa. Saba and I now shared the lions' story, while I continued to follow the leopards and Simon the cheetahs. But for the fifth series, I asked if I could take over the cheetahs, with Angie as one of our spotters, as by then we were working on this book and were keen to spend as much

time with the cheetahs as possible. So it was decided that Simon should work with the Marsh Lions. With such a large pride – two males, six females and 16 cubs – we would need a second camera, and as Simon is a cameraman as well as a presenter he was the ideal person for the job. That meant that I could follow the cheetah story, and Saba would take the leopards. I would also try to discover what had happened to Solo, a charismatic young male lion who had been one of the stars of series three.

In 2000, Solo was the only small cub in the Ridge Pride, southern neighbours of the Marsh Pride. He had enchanted us with his playful antics and was a rich source of entertainment for his older siblings. I felt sure that he would not survive the rigours of the rainy season, when the wildebeest and zebras retreat across the border into the Serengeti National Park in Tanzania. Whenever food is in short supply, it is the young cubs who suffer most, and many – 50 per cent or more – disappear. But Solo survived, and two years later had grown into a feisty young male. By this time two new adult males had moved into the area, possibly nomads from as far afield as the Serengeti, feasting off the bounty represented by the migration and

disrupting the harmony of the Ridge Pride. They ousted the two old Ridge Pride males, Solo's father and uncle, and drove Solo and a slightly older male relative – along with a number of other subadults – out of the pride. On his own, Solo would have stood little chance of survival, but together the two young males managed to eke out a living, brawling with older pride mates and warring with the local hyena clans for food, while steering well clear of the Serengeti males.

But that had all been a year ago. Where were Solo and his companion now? If we were lucky we might still find them out there somewhere, but it was far more likely that they would have moved on, destined to wander as nomads for another year or so – if they survived – until they were four or five years old and sufficiently battle-hardened to take over a pride of females and sire cubs of their own. Though the largest prides in the Mara are accompanied by coalitions of three or even four males, more than half have only two, so Solo and his companion had a good chance of success.

I felt almost guilty turning my back on the leopard story after all my years of searching, day in day out, for the most enigmatic and secretive of cats. To confound expectations, on the cheetah crew's first game drive, Angie spotted a beautiful young male leopard wandering along the edge of the riverine forest between Governor's Camp and Paradise Plain. We stopped to watch him as he paused every so often to arch his long spotted tail, spraying a shower of scent to mark the bushes and fallen trees that lined the game paths he knew so well, signifying to every other leopard that this was his territory. We called Saba on the radio, but by the time she arrived the male had disappeared into the undergrowth. In recent years leopards have become much easier to find throughout the Mara, and in the area where we film there are a number whom the drivers and guides now see often enough to know where best to search for them and to have recorded details of their history.

How different things are now to when I first came to the Mara. In the 1970s, months would pass without a hint of a spotted coat disappearing through the grass, and so it remained until a leopard called the Paradise female (later renamed Half-Tail) emerged from the shadows along Fig Tree Ridge and Leopard Gorge in the late 1980s. In 1996, Half-Tail and her daughter Zawadi (Shadow to *BCD* viewers) stole the show, and even when Half-Tail was killed in a snare set by Masai herdsmen in retaliation for a stock-raiding incident in early 1999, Zawadi was there to enthral us, providing some unforgettable moments when she had cubs of her own in 2000 and 2002. At that time there was no other leopard as habituated to vehicles as she was, nor could you hope to find a more photogenic setting than Fig Tree Ridge and Leopard Gorge to film a leopard with cubs. But by 2003 our luck had finally run out. Hard as the game spotters searched, nobody could find any trace of Zawadi in her usual haunts, nor could we locate her daughter Safi, who had reared a cub along the Olare Orok Lugga to the east of Leopard Gorge.

Part of the problem was that concerns about worldwide terrorism and general security meant that far fewer tourists visited the Mara – during the last few years the number of visitors to Kenya has dropped from more than 900,000 to less than 400,000. As a result, there were fewer vehicles out searching for big cats. The closure of Mara River Camp, where I was based from 1977 to 1981, also had an impact. The camp had become a popular venue for photographers who would always be on the lookout for Zawadi, helping us to keep track of her movements. Now that source of information was gone.

By the time the long rains had petered out in June, much of the area was shrouded beneath a blanket of tall grass, so finding a leopard was always going to be difficult,

even a leopard as vehicle-friendly as Zawadi. We were despondent. Everybody loved Zawadi, and she had featured in all the previous series; we had been able to watch as she transformed from a boisterous

Zawadi is so tolerant of vehicles that she acts as if they do not exist. Recently she has shifted her territory further west, and is seen less often along Fig Tree Ridge and Leopard Gorge.

seven-month-old cub into a strikingly elegant adult. By now she was seven years old and in her prime, though she had raised just one cub – Safi – out of ten offspring from the four litters she had

Zawadi gave birth to her fifth litter shortly after this photograph was taken. The two cubs are now large enough to follow her to a kill and we hope to film them later in the year.

conceived since beginning to breed at the age of three.

We couldn't help smiling to ourselves when Zawadi was located the day after we finished filming. There she was, as relaxed as ever, resting near a kill in the western-most part of her home range bordering the Mara River; it typified so exactly the elusive nature of *all* leopards. There was no sign that she had dependent cubs, but it was nice to know that she was still in good health, living her life hidden from view, perhaps enjoying a brief respite from all the attention that she normally received from vehicles.

With so little time to film *Big Cat Week*, the pressure was intense for all of us, though none more so than for the leopard crew. After a week of frustration Saba and her team abandoned the search for Zawadi and switched their attentions to another

leopard, who three months earlier had given birth to two cubs along the Talek River, a good hour's drive to the east of our camp. In the end the decision to concentrate on Bella, as she became known, was fully justified, and cameraman Gordon Buchanan, who had worked with leopards in Sri Lanka, managed to get some beautiful shots of her and her cubs. I had watched Bella while staying at the nearby Mara Intrepids Camp with a group of photographers in April, just a month or so before she gave birth. I knew the moment I saw her that she was a leopard I had watched before. Bigger and stockier than Zawadi, she had very distinctive eyes that looked as if someone had painted a dark line of mascara along her upper eyelids. We had filmed her briefly resting in a fig tree along the banks of the Talek River in 2000, accompanied by a six-month-old cub. At

the time we had been searching for Zawadi and Safi after they disappeared for nearly three weeks following an altercation with a male known as Droopy Jaw. We were desperate to find another leopard we could work with in case Zawadi failed to turn up again. In the end we didn't need to – but now we certainly did.

The Talek has always been superb leopard country. There is plenty of cover, and a number of magnificent fig trees line the banks of the river where a leopard can rest up or stash its kill. Fallen trees spread like sculpted figurines across the riverbed, offering perfect hiding places for a mother leopard with small cubs. In addition to this, Mara Intrepids Camp regularly puts out bait for leopards on the far bank of the river. opposite a platform where visitors gather in the evening for sundowners in the hope of catching a glimpse of the cat that walks alone. They are rarely disappointed, with up to four leopards coming to feed on the bait during the evening. Some people question the propriety of baiting for leopards, but I see nothing wrong in it. Leopards are not going to stop hunting just because someone puts out a leg of meat for them – though the Masai could feel that providing a goat or sheep carcass for leopards might encourage them to take livestock when they wander outside the reserve. In fact leopards are such superb hunters that they can usually find more than enough to eat among the wild game, though subadults dispersing from their natal range might pose a problem for the pastoralists, as could old leopards.

Bella proved a worthy replacement for Zawadi, although the area where she lives is much tougher for vehicles to negotiate – which made it easier for Bella to keep a low profile when she chose. During the month the crew followed her, they gradually learned her routine – where she liked to lie up during the day, where to search for her cubs, her favourite ambush sites. On one memorable occasion she killed three wildebeest calves in a single day as the herds came down to drink and cross the Talek River. The Talek is also a good place to search for lions, so Bella kept her cubs carefully hidden during the first few months, though there were occasions when Gordon was able to photograph mother and cubs as they suckled, groomed and played in the sandy riverbed.

Closer to our camp, along the Bila Shaka Lugga at the heart of the Marsh Pride's territory, Simon had plenty to keep him busy – the pride had swollen to 29 lions, thanks to the addition of another five cubs since we had last filmed them a year earlier. These were exciting times to be watching the Marsh Lions. Trouble had been brewing for the pride for a while in the robust form of two young nomadic males. Angie and I had met them one morning a week earlier as they lay on their haunches, looking acquisitively down on the Marsh Pride's

A buffalo kill provides a pride of lions with a sizeable meal, though only large prides can tackle such dangerous prey.

territory with the keen interest of lions hungry for a place to call their own. Something was amiss with the Marsh Lions and the two young males knew it. This was the chance they had been waiting for. One of the pride males – the older and larger of the two Blond Males who had taken over the territory three and a half years earlier – had been fatally gored by a buffalo. Buffaloes are powerful creatures, armed with massive hook-like horns that can smash the life from any lion who does not proceed with the utmost caution. Battles between the two are often titanic affairs – the power of numbers pitted against brute strength and endless courage. The pride had attacked a cantankerous old bull at night near the spring that is the perennial lifeblood of Musiara Marsh, the lions' dry-season hunting ground. Though they eventually managed to subdue him, they were to pay a heavy price. The death of the older pride male left his companion Simba in an unenviable position. A single male lion can never hope to hold a territory in the Mara for long. There are just too many bands of

One of the Blond Males mating with a Marsh Pride lioness. He was later killed by buffaloes, leaving his companion to struggle to maintain control of the pride alone.

young nomads waiting for the chance to take over a pride, quite apart from the threat posed by males from adjacent areas, always ready to take advantage of any weakening of a neighbour's ability to defend his territory in order to expand their realm of influence.

Male lions have such a powerful aura. There is an arrogance to the way they saunter purposefully about their business, a visible expression of confidence in their own capabilities, and never more so than when there is a dispute over territory. The two nomads were ready to make their move. By the time filming was over they had forced Simba to abandon his favourite resting places along Bila Shaka, prompting the lionesses to flee with their young to the safety of Musiara Marsh. There was a strange irony to what was happening, a sense of life repeating itself, of the old order being replaced by the new. Three years earlier the Blond Males had

Scar with one of Khali's ten-week-old cubs; she lost this litter to the Blond Males when they took over the Marsh Pride's territory and forced Scar to flee for his life.

abandoned the females of the Topi Plains pride – which claims the area to the east of Bila Shaka – in response to the death of Scruffy, the Marsh male who had been killed by Masai herdsmen in a cattle incident in December 1999. This had left his companion Scar to try to hold the Marsh Pride territory on his own.

Scar was a magnificent male, with a huge, tobacco-coloured mane that extended down across his broad chest, making him visible from far away on the open plains. But now that Scar was alone, the only advantage his mane brought him was as a shield from the blows of his adversaries. He clung on for a while by hiding out among the dense reedbeds of the marsh, living off the proceeds of kills made by the remnants of his pride – just as Simba was now forced to do. Some of the adult lionesses had already returned to the Bila Shaka Lugga and mated with the new males, but for Scar there was no going back. Most male lions die a violent death, either killed by a new generation of pride males or forced from their territory to survive as best they can among the hyenas and the Masai. Old and weary, ravaged by the cumulative effect of wounds and disease, there is no easy end. Scar was one of the fortunate ones. He had sired many

cubs during his long tenure as a pride male, the objective of any lion's existence.

When we embarked on the fourth series of *BCD* in 2002, the six Marsh lionesses born in 1998 were no longer exiles. As they matured, they had returned to the Bila Shaka Lugga and mated with the Blond Males. There were now eight adult lionesses in the pride, including two old females whom Angie and I had named Khali (the angry one) and Notch – the grandmothers of the pride. We watched as three of the lionesses gave birth at about the same time,

establishing a crèche of eleven cubs. With so many mouths to feed, the pride became increasingly fragmented and I couldn't help thinking that we might soon see a split, as the Marsh Pride's territory normally supports only four to six lionesses. But by targeting large prey such as buffaloes and giraffes – something that smaller prides rarely do – the Marsh pride managed to remain intact.

In fact, although the eleven cubs survived, the tensions we had noticed developing between the lionesses were still in evidence when Khali's daughter Bibi produced her first litter a few weeks before filming of *Big Cat Week* began. Having failed to conceive at the same time as her pride mates, she was not part of the crèche that had developed a year earlier. Instead, she found herself an object of hostility to most of the other members of her pride. Yet she had no alternative but to cling to her familiar range. She had been born along the Bila Shaka Lugga five years earlier, so it was only natural that she should now choose the same place to have her cubs. It was better for her to stay in her territory than to face an uncertain future among neighbouring prides.

By the time Simon and cameraman Warwick Schlöss began filming, Bibi and

White-Eye of the Marsh Pride showing her displeasure at being pestered for milk not only by her own offspring but by Khali and Mama Lugga's cubs, part of a crèche of eleven youngsters.

her two five-week-old cubs were being seen regularly along the Bila Shaka Lugga; at one point the tiny kittens were cornered by the older generation of Marsh cubs and had to endure a playful mauling from their relatives. Bibi had fled when the pride moved in, perhaps hoping that in her absence the others might leave her cubs alone. Not only was she now ostracized by most of the females in the Marsh Pride, she had the added burdens of attempting to raise her cubs in isolation and of trying to avoid the new males.

And so to the cheetahs. I couldn't have imagined a more perfect scenario for filming. By good fortune a young cheetah we had named Kike (Swahili for 'young female') had given birth to four cubs in December 2002. Kike was as much a favourite with the drivers as Half-Tail the leopard and her contemporary Amber the cheetah had been. In fact she was believed to be one of Amber's daughters – though not, as we first suspected, the female cub that Simon had filmed in 1998, the only female in a litter of three tearaway youngsters. That young female had eventually settled in the Mara Intrepids and Rhino Ridge area. We filmed her for a *BCD* update in 1999, when she climbed onto the roof of my vehicle, and again in 2000 scrapping with Nick, the territorial male, leaving him with blood dripping from his nose. But despite her ability to defend herself, she was painfully thin and looked in poor health, even taking into account a cheetah's naturally slim-line physique. As far as we know she never managed to raise cubs, and she disappeared from her home range some time in late 2000.

In July 2002 Angie was told about a young female cheetah who had given birth to four cubs along the Bila Shaka Lugga, dangerously close to where the Marsh Lions so often lie up. This area has been a cemetery for cheetah cubs over the years, as whenever a female succumbs to the temptation to give birth along the lugga or in the long marshy grass bordering it, the

lions inevitably find and kill them. I witnessed such an incident shortly after I first came to live in the Mara. A tour vehicle rushed forward as the lions chased the cheetah mother away and killed two of her cubs, and even though the car then stood guard until the mother eventually returned, the two surviving cubs disappeared shortly afterwards.

We were concerned that something similar might happen to the cubs that Angie had been told about. Vehicles were driving so close to the den that one little girl dropped a pair of binoculars among the cubs, and we feared that all the traffic would alert the lions to the cheetahs' presence. Sensing a disaster in the making, Angie called Dr Richard Leakey, former

Khali watches intently as the Blond Males try to find her hiding place. In the end they tracked the cubs down, killed them and were able to mate with the lioness.

head of the Kenya Wildlife Service; through Governor's Camp and the Narok County Council he organized for a vehicle to ensure the cheetahs weren't harassed. But by now the lions were barely 50m (160ft) from the den, and sure enough they must have become suspicious when they saw a female cheetah moving cautiously around the area. Early one morning, one of the Blond Males found the cubs and killed them. All our hopes of filming that particular family evaporated, and neither Amber nor Kike had cubs. So Simon and cameraman Warren Samuels decided to concentrate on the Mara Triangle, where two female cheetahs were regularly being seen, each with three cubs. One litter was four months old, the other six, and Simon decided to concentrate on the mother with the younger cubs, whom he named Honey.

Young cheetah cubs are delightful to watch; these were large enough to follow their mother and full of fun and games, providing us with plenty of action. There were the inevitable confrontations with predators, and one particularly nail-biting encounter with a full-grown male lion which prompted Honey to challenge him, giving her cubs vital seconds to run away. Cliff-hangers such as this help to make *BCD* so popular with viewers, with everyone desperately wanting to know whether or not the cubs would survive.

Just before we finished filming at the end of 2002, a third female gave birth to five cubs. Tracking the fate of the three litters provided a stark reminder of how difficult it is for cheetahs to raise cubs in the Mara–Serengeti.

Amber finally disappeared in early 2003. But just as Half-Tail had seemingly emerged from nowhere when she first appeared around Leopard Gorge in the late 1980s as a two-year-old, so too did Kike arrive from out of the blue. We had all thought that Amber had a remarkable temperament: apparently indifferent to whatever was happening around her and pointedly ignoring the people craning their necks out of the roof-hatches to take her picture, she would stare into the distance, more concerned with simply being a cheetah, searching for signs of young gazelles or other suitable prey to hunt, or for danger in the form of hyenas and lions.

Kike took the habituation process a step further. No sooner had she leapt onto the bonnet of a vehicle than she would bend forward, carefully sniffing around for scent. Invariably it was her own scent that she detected and she would quickly douse the spot with urine so concentrated that it left a pattern of crystals like snowflakes – this

Honey and one of her five-month-old cubs in September 2002. Every cheetah has different spot markings, with the patterns on the face, chest and tail being good points of reference.

Kike uses vehicles as if they were termite mounds. From up here she has an unimpeded view and can search for prey and keep watch for danger.

had been a part of Amber's ritual, too. Then Kike would crouch and leap up onto the roof, pausing to sniff around each hatch, depositing two or even three piles of exceptionally smelly faeces as her calling card. At times the smell was so overpowering that I would be embarrassed when another vehicle drove over for a chat – it wouldn't be long before people started to grimace at the stench.

Under other circumstances the last thing one would wish for would be a big cat climbing onto one's car. I once had a full-grown lioness leap onto the bonnet of a vehicle while we were filming in the Ngorongoro Crater. It was an uncomfortable experience having all the roof-hatches open and no chance of closing them without scaring the 120kg (265lb) cat and provoking an incident. As for leopards, they are without doubt the most volatile and unpredictable of Africa's three big cats, and there have been a number of incidents over the years in which an angry leopard has charged a vehicle and leapt inside with potentially serious repercussions for the occupants. But a cheetah is a very different kind of cat.

Kike provided Angie and me with the opportunity to observe a wild creature up closer than we had ever done before. She broke all the boundaries that one normally associates with big cats. Her acceptance of vehicles was so complete and trusting that we were able to see her in a very different light by comparison to our encounters with lions and leopards, and gain a clearer understanding of the true nature of these remarkable creatures. It was easy to see why man was able to semi-domesticate cheetahs for hunting purposes. They may look too fragile to compete with the other predators in their fight for survival, but they are braver and tougher than they look. Their method of hunting by means of a high-speed chase makes them the last of the sprinting cats. They are indeed a revelation.

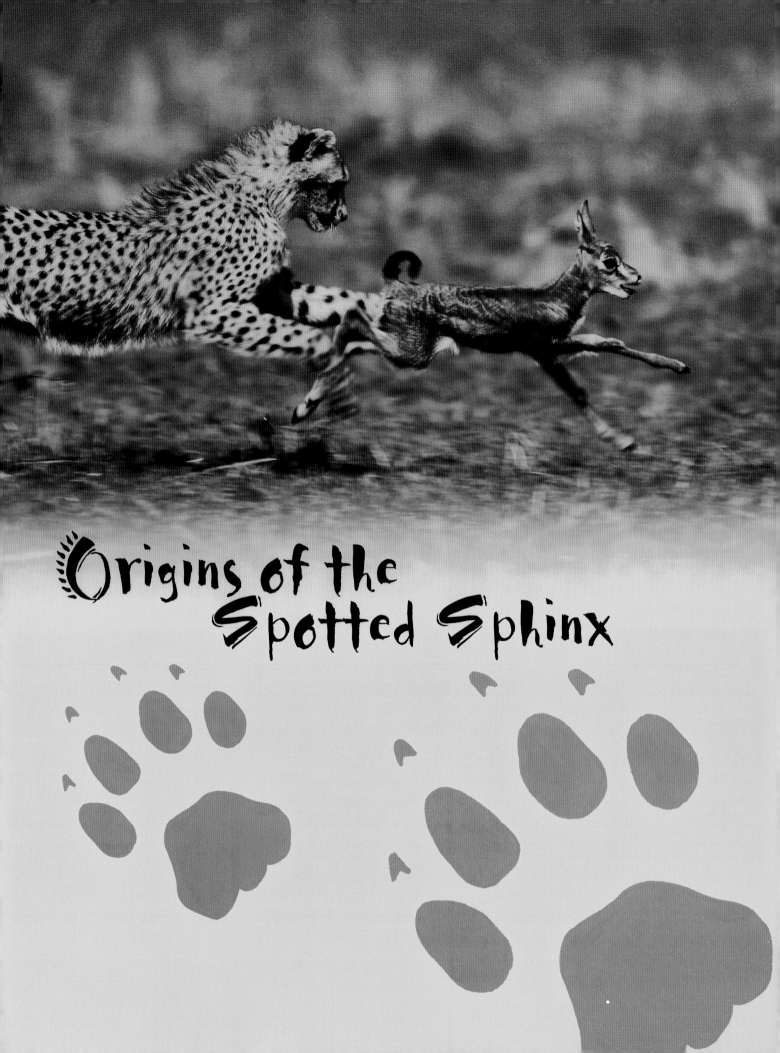

Origins of the Spotted Sphinx

It is tempting to think of lions, leopards and cheetahs as typically African animals – all three seem so much a part of the African landscape, merging with the colours of golden grass and dappled savanna. Yet they were a constant feature of Asia and Europe in times past, and lions and cheetahs were once found in North America, too. Both are still represented by Asian subspecies that formerly occurred throughout the Middle East, across central Asia and down into India. But just as the Asiatic lion now exists only as a relic population of about 300 in India's Gir Forest, so the cheetah clings on, with perhaps 60 individuals still found in Iran, and the occasional cat in western Pakistan. The depletion of the cheetah's natural prey – the blackbuck in India and gazelles on the Arabian Peninsula – through hunting and habitat loss has been a major reason for its decline, as has the hunting of cheetahs for sport and their pelt.

With so few Asiatic cheetahs remaining it is difficult to determine how – if at all – it differs from the African cheetah, which is known to be highly inbred. It is said to be

Cheetahs hunt at any time of the day – and occasionally at night. They normally try to avoid contact with lions and hyenas by hunting when the larger predators have lain up for the day.

slightly larger than its African cousin, with a lighter coloured but thicker coat and a more prominent neck ruff.

In Africa the cheetah is known historically from 38 countries. It once ranged through all parts of the continent bar desert and tropical forest, from the Mediterranean to the Cape of Good Hope. Today it occurs in 29 countries and is most widespread in grassy plains, open woodlands and semi-desert. Its North and

Western African range has shrunk to just a few individuals in the southern Saharan mountain regions, with 300–500 surviving in the Sahara, principally in Mali, Niger and Chad. As we shall see in Chapter 7, Namibia is the last real cheetah stronghold, with perhaps 3,000 individuals, and healthy populations also exist in Tanzania, Kenya (less than 1,000), Botswana (1,500), Zimbabwe (1,500) and South Africa (700).

As recently as the early 1990s, seven subspecies were recognized, though the discovery that cheetahs from geographically isolated populations in eastern and southern Africa were genetically almost identical means that throughout this region at least splitting them into subspecies may be questionable. However, recent studies on cheetahs from northern Somalia show them to be clearly distinguishable genetically from Namibian cheetahs. Experts currently divide the population into five subspecies:

Acinonyx jubatus venaticus – Asiatic cheetah, found in Iran, Egypt, Algeria and the northern Sahara.

A. j. hecki – West African cheetah: Benin, Burkina Faso, Mali, Mauritania, Niger and Senegal.

A. j. soemmeringii – Central African cheetah: Cameroon, Chad, Central African Republic, Ethiopia, Nigeria (may be extinct), southern Niger, northern Somalia and Sudan.

Honey and her four-month-old cubs in the Mara Triangle. This is one of the best places in Africa to see cheetahs – there are plenty of Thomson's gazelles for them to prey on.

A. j. raineyii – East African cheetah: Kenya, central and northern Tanzania, southern Somalia and Uganda.

A. j. jubatus – Southern African cheetah: Angola, Botswana, Congo, Malawi, Mozambique, South Africa, southern Tanzania, Zambia and Zimbabwe.

The so-called 'king' cheetah (once considered a separate species and known as *Acinonyx rex*), with its beautiful pattern of serval-like streaks and blotches along its back, is now known to be merely a colour variation: it possesses a pair of recessive genes for coat pattern identical to those of *A. jubatus*. Kings can be born among a litter conceived by a pair of cheetahs with the usual pattern of spots, though a pair of kings can produce only cubs with king markings. Kings were first identified from a small region around north-eastern South Africa, Zimbabwe and eastern Botswana. More recently a skin was recovered from a poacher in Burkina Faso, indicating that the mutation occurs more widely.

The origins of the cat or felid family are plagued by a lack of fossil remains. We do know that cats first appeared around 30 million years ago (mya) in Europe, branching off from the miacids, the earliest

carnivores, which probably looked and behaved like genets. The first known cat was *Proailurus*, which means 'early cat'; it was the size of an ocelot and bore the distinctive cheek teeth or carnassials that characterize members of the order Carnivora. Some 20 mya a new genus of cats known as *Pseudaelurus* appeared in Eurasia. This was a time when some of the world's forested regions were being replaced by more open country, leading to an explosion in grass- and seed-eating animals and to a diversification in the number and kinds of cats that preyed on them, some of which could run like the wind. *Pseudaelurus* crossed the landbridge that appeared between Eurasia and Africa as ocean levels dropped about this period, bringing cats to Africa for the first time.

Around 15 mya *Pseudaelurus* gave rise to two distinct lineages, one of which produced the modern cats, including the cheetah, the other the fabled sabre-tooths. The latter appeared both in the Americas and in Africa, though the African species died out long before the Californian *Smilodon*, which went extinct only around 9,500 years ago. But 3 mya there were at least three species of sabre-tooths living in

Africa at the same time as the lion, leopard and cheetah.

Paleoecological records show that at least four species of cheetah-like cats ranged across Asia, Africa and North America as little as 10,000 years ago. If the fossil evidence is to be believed, the modern cheetah is an Old World species, with at least two other Old World cheetahs possibly existing at the same time. One of them was the giant European cheetah (*Acinonyx pardinensis*), which may have occurred as much as 3.8 mya (earlier than has been suggested by molecular studies); the other was the smaller *A. intermedius*, which ranged across Europe and as far east as China from the mid-Pleistocene, around 1 mya.

One problem for taxonomists is that many of the modern cat species almost certainly once had a far more extensive distribution than they do today. The scarcity of cheetah fossils mirrors its solitary and far-ranging habits, with the number in any given area being relatively small. It seems that the cheetah has been sparsely distributed from the start. While the European cheetah was hunting the open grasslands in the western part of its

'Tommies' are the fastest of the antelopes and gazelles found in East Africa, reaching speeds of 65kph (40mph). In the Mara–Serengeti they are the main prey of cheetahs and wild dogs.

range approximately 1–3 mya, a similarly large cheetah is known from fossil deposits in India and China, and may well be the same animal. Skull fragments of several European cheetahs dating back approximately 2.1 million years have been discovered at Saint-Vallier, on the east side of the Rhone Valley in France, and this species is known to have survived until at least 500,000 years ago at the German site of Mosbach. Weighing 95kg (210lb) and standing 90cm (3ft) at the shoulder, the European cheetah would have been almost double the size and weight of its modern relative and must have been an impressive sight as it sprinted after its prey.

The best collection of skeletal bones from the European cheetah comes from Perrier in the Massif Central of France, where long bones and much of the vertebral column from one individual have been located. These finds confirm that the European cheetah was just as specialized a sprinter as the modern one, possessing the typical long back and elongated limbs that would have allowed it to pursue antelope and deer at high speeds. It may not have been quite as fast as today's cheetah, which is probably the optimal size for maximum speed. Like the cave lion that inhabited Europe from around 700,000 years ago, the European cheetah decreased in size during the middle Pleistocene, so that by the late Pleistocene, 500,000 years ago, the fossil forms are very similar to the recent species.

It seems likely that the European cheetah had longer, denser fur than its living relative to compensate for the colder climate in the more northerly part of its range, and that it developed a winter coat in the same manner as leopards and tigers do today in China and Siberia, giving it a stockier appearance. Some people feel that *A. pardinensis* and *A. jubatus* might logically be considered a single species, with the larger size of the more northerly form partly explained by the fact that members of the same species are often larger in colder climates, as a bigger body conserves heat better.

Many fleet-footed or cursorial predators were also found in North America as the Ice Age drew to a close in the late Pleistocene. Remains of one cat, *Miracinonyx trumani*, discovered in Wyoming and dating from around 11,000 years ago, are strikingly similar to the modern cheetah. Initially classified as *Felis trumani*, it was later thought to be a more cursorial predator than is typical for felids, so some taxonomists include it in the same genus as the modern cheetah, describing it as *Acinonyx trumani*, rather than placing it in the subgenus *Miracinonyx*.

An even more ancient cheetah-like cat, *Miracinonyx inexpectatus*, existed in North America perhaps as far back as 3.2 mya and was similar in size to the large European cheetah. An early, almost complete skeleton from Hamilton Cave in Virginia reveals body proportions intermediate between the puma and modern cheetah, with a shortened, domed skull, enlarged nasal openings and rather short canine teeth – as in the living cheetah – but with less elongated lower limbs and claws that are fully concealed when retracted (the cheetah's claws are not covered by a sheath when retracted, unlike those of other cats, who need to keep their claws sharp for hunting and climbing). The impression is of a versatile cat, faster than a puma, stronger and better suited to climbing than a cheetah, with a shoulder height of 85cm (34in) and a possible weight of up to 95kg (210lb).

Kike in full flight. Cheetahs are the fastest animal on four legs over a short distance, though they cannot sustain a high speed for more than a few hundred metres.

The king cheetah is not a separate species – its beautiful coat markings are produced by a recessive gene for coat colour.

Even more significant, perhaps, is the fact that both *Miracinonyx* and the modern cheetah lack a post-canine gap, a feature present only in the cheetah among living cats, pointing perhaps to a common descent. This would place North America as the cheetah's centre of evolution. Some taxonomists think that *Miracinonyx* might be more closely allied to the puma, possibly even ancestral to it, though like the cheetah – but unlike other cats – it also has reduced infraorbital foramina (small openings in the skull), which in the cheetah are associated with shortened whiskers and reflect the fact

that the cheetah is less nocturnal than most other cats. It is possible then that both cheetah and puma descended from a common ancestor among the *Pseudaeluri*, with the cheetah dispersing from North America across Asia and on into Africa.

Many experts still find the cheetah an enigma. As recently as ten years ago it was referred to by taxonomists as *incertae sedis* – of undetermined lineage – among the members of the cat family Felidae. All other cats are grouped in two subfamilies known as the Pantherinae, ranging in size from the tiger to the caracal, and the Felinae, from pumas to black-footed cats. However, recent work in the field of molecular genetics, using analysis of a species' DNA, has created a new and exciting yardstick for measuring relatedness and clarifying evolutionary relationships. Based on these findings, it appears that the 36 species of modern cats have evolved within the past 10–15 million years from eight recognizable lineages: Ocelot, Domestic cat, Puma, Leopard cat, Panthera, Lynx, Caracal and Bay cat. And as some people had thought based on the fossil evidence, the cheetah is indeed part of the Puma lineage, which links it to the puma and the taxonomic puzzle the jaguarundi, the most

widely distributed and commonly seen cat in Central and South America. It is a strange-looking creature, more like a martin, weasel or otter than a cat, with short legs, a slender body, a long tail and a sleek, uniformly coloured coat of either iron-grey or red-brown. If you had to hazard a guess as to the jaguarundi's nearest living relative, you certainly wouldn't say a puma or a cheetah, proving what a powerful tool the new discipline of molecular genetics is. Although closely related to the puma, the jaguarundi shares a more distant association with the cheetah, which diverged from the three cats' common ancestor some 8.25 mya.

Though both the puma and cheetah are 'big cats' in size, they are distinct from members of the *Panthera* lineage, which includes the other two African big cats, the lion and leopard, along with the jaguar, tiger, snow leopard and clouded leopard. The clouded leopard was first to diverge from their common ancestor, followed by the snow leopard. The four others, who make up today's genus *Panthera* – the roaring cats – diverged most recently, 2 to 3 mya. But quite how and when the various branches emerged is still in question, and the existence of fossil records for lions and leopards dating back 3.5 mya in Africa highlights the fact that while molecular genetics is vital in assessing relationships between the different cat species it is by no means infallible in establishing timing.

While the Puma lineage seems the rightful home for the cheetah, the oldest fossils of the modern cheetah place it in East Africa around 3.5 mya, which hints at an African genesis. To quote biologist Dr Luke Hunter:

The cheetah as we know it may have first evolved in Africa from an earlier species on the cheetah-puma branch which had arisen elsewhere and colonized Africa. Then, shortly after its appearance in Africa 3.5 mya, the

The jaguarundi is the most widely distributed and commonly seen cat in Central and South America and, along with the puma, is the cheetah's closest relative.

The modern cheetah's scientific name, Acinonyx jubatus, derives from the Greek words akineo (no movement) or akaina (thorn) and onyx (claw), referring to its more visible claws – and from the Latin jubatus, meaning possessing a crest or mane. Its English name comes from chita, Hindi for spotted one. The cheetah is unique among the cats in combining the explosive power of the felids with the pursuit tactics of dogs. Comparisons with members of the dog family seem apt, since the cheetah has the athletic build and sprinting ability of a greyhound, yet there is no doubting that it is very much a cat. Anyone fortunate enough to have spent time close to a wild cheetah – or a tame one, for that matter – may have heard the loud purring of contentment from a mother and her cubs as they huddle within touching distance of one another in some shady spot out on the African savanna. Although, as we shall see, vocalizations do play a role in cheetah communication, especially between a mother and her cubs, what the cheetah cannot do is roar. It lacks the large fibrous pads on the vocal chords that are thought to be the reason the big cats of the genus Panthera – the lion, tiger, leopard and jaguar – can roar but not purr.

Honey, like all cheetah mothers, was always on the look-out for danger, particularly from lions, hyenas and leopards.

modern cheetah could have spread rapidly throughout Eurasia while other cheetah species were evolving elsewhere in the world, possibly from the same distant ancestor that gave rise to the African cheetah.

Seemingly, then, the cheetah's origins remain something of a mystery, not least because of nature's habit of evolving similar designs among unrelated species. This process, referred to as parallel evolution, has been put forward as a possible explanation for some of the cheetah-like fossils found in North America, in the same way that sabre-tooths evolved on a number of occasions among quite unrelated animals. To add to the confusion, all cats, from the 1kg (2lb) black-footed cat of southern Africa to the 225kg (500lb) tiger, are basically of a similar design. Individuals within a single species may differ enormously – leopards, for example, vary in size from 90kg (200lb) on the forested slopes of Mount Kenya to 30kg (65lb) in the Cape Mountains of South Africa. At first

sight you might be forgiven for thinking they were separate species, but they are not – the disparity in size merely reflects adaptations to life under different climatic and habitat conditions, and to the type and size of prey available to them. Conversely, the similarities between *Acinonyx* and *Miracinonyx* may prove to be a case of parallel evolution, with the various forms of fleet-footed, prong-horned antelope perhaps determining the path of the North American cheetah's evolution.

Cheetahs have historically shared a closer relationship with humans than any of the other big cats. Man has tamed them both as symbols of speed and elegance and to hunt antelope for sport and prestige, in a connection that dates back at least 4,000–5,000 years. So how did this relationship evolve? Two million years ago, when our human ancestors left the forests and began to wander into the emerging savannas of Africa, they would have found the cheetah already there, joining a guild of predators and scavengers that included lions, leopards and hyenas as we know

them today. Lions must have been terrifying competitors for our ancestors, but not cheetahs. By forming clans or family groups, we would have been able to counter the greater power of lions; so too would we have dominated the fragile-looking cheetah and driven it from its kill – just as baboons sometimes do. I have seen them chase a mother cheetah and her large cubs from a freshly killed topi calf before the cats had time to satisfy their hunger. Humans fear the dark, so being able to intimidate a cat that hunted by day would have offered the ideal chance of acquiring a freshly killed carcass in open terrain, to supplement our diet of fruit, leaves, berries and roots. The Bushmen of the central Kalahari are well aware of this and will take a fresh kill from a cheetah simply by walking up to it, waving their arms and shouting to force the cat to back off.

The cheetah's visibility and our ancestors' knowledge of the way it hunted would have contributed to the next step – catching, taming and using it for sport. The risk of injury would have been far less than trying to manhandle a lion or a leopard, both of which remain unpredictable all their life and have the power to kill a human adversary. The cheetah proved an ideal hunting companion and was used for coursing in Asia prior to the Assyrian dynasty, about 1300 BC; in Libya two thousand years ago during the reign of the Pharaohs (who believed that the fleet-footed cheetah would spirit their soul away after death); and by Mogul emperors in India between the 13th and 16th centuries. A silver ornament retrieved from a burial mound in the Caucasus dates to between 700 and 300 BC and shows cheetahs wearing collars, and a Mesopotamian seal from as early as the third millennium BC depicts a cheetah-like cat on a leash. Many Egyptian tombs and rock temples bear the mark of the cheetah, and some of the earliest depictions of training and using cheetahs for hunting come from the 17th and 18th dynasties in Egypt, about 1700–1500 BC.

The practice of hunting with cheetahs spread throughout the Middle East, Afghanistan, southern Russia, Pakistan, India and China, and was primarily the preserve of the rich and famous. Tame cheetahs were used to hunt goitered gazelles, foxes and hares in Russia and Mongolia, and the sport flourished during the Middle Ages in Azerbaijan, Armenia and Georgia. In 1474 one Armenian ruler owned a hundred hunting cheetahs.

Cheetahs are relatively easy to catch. Isolated in open country, they are no match for a band of men on horses, or for a pack of dogs. Their strength lies in a short, high-speed chase, sufficient to catch their prey and keep them safe from lions, leopards and hyenas. But when pursued by an adversary with stamina and guile the cheetah is doomed, winded by the chase after a few hundred metres. Its world is based on its pin-sharp vision; escape, defence and hunting are centred on sight. Once a cheetah was cornered, the key to restraining it was quickly to place a hood over its eyes, robbing it of its primary sense.

Instilling a dependence on humans was also easy. Hand-feeding was the answer, as I saw for myself on a visit to a game ranch in Namibia, where newly captured subadult cheetahs quickly quietened down and accepted – or rather snatched – chunks of meat offered to them through the ventilation holes in their box traps. Try doing that with a wild lion or leopard and you are liable to lose your hand, quite apart from being frightened to death by their grunts and roars of fear and anger.

The most prominent practitioner of this ancient sport was Akbar the Great, the 16th-century Mogul emperor and ruler of what is now northern India, Pakistan and Afghanistan. He is said to have kept a thousand cheetahs in his menagerie and was certainly the first Indian potentate to use them for hunting, after being presented with a cat named Fatehbaz in 1555. During his 49-year reign Akbar reportedly collected over 9,000 cheetahs – nearly a seventh of today's world population – hunting gazelles and antelope with them, and helping to create a culture that survived until the middle of the 20th century.

The reason Akbar captured so many cheetahs was that they proved almost impossible to breed in captivity, despite being accorded the freedom of the palace grounds. He managed to breed from a cheetah only once, when a male slipped his collar and mated with a female who later gave birth to three cubs, all of whom survived to adulthood. Accounts of the sheer number of cheetahs kept by Akbar

A mother cheetah begins releasing young gazelles to her cubs when they are four months old, allowing them to practise their hunting skills.

hint at their relative abundance in Asia until comparatively recently.

Coursing in Europe with cheetahs imported from Africa spanned nearly a thousand years and was surrounded by grandeur. In 1231, Frederick the Great of Prussia went to Ravenna in Italy accompanied by a court that contained bodyguards, astrologers, huntsmen and falconers, and a menagerie including elephants, dromedaries, camels, falcons and cheetahs. The popularity of cheetah hunting reached its peak in the 14th and 15th centuries in Italy, France and England, with wealthy landowners and royalty spending a small fortune on acquiring and keeping these elegant hunting cats to run down hares and roe deer. Cheetahs are depicted in paintings and tapestries being carried to the hunt on horseback, seated on a pillow behind the handler, while in India they were transported in ox wagons, hooded like a falcon until they were within striking distance of their quarry. It soon became apparent to the handlers that you needed to catch adult cheetahs. Cubs who had not learned the necessary hunting skills from their mother were far harder to train. Indian princes were still using cheetahs to hunt blackbuck in 1929, but by then the Asiatic population was so drastically reduced that these too were imported from Africa. The last of India's cheetahs – three young males sitting by the roadside – were shot in 1947.

With cheetahs being so superbly adapted to their hunting way of life, it is worth pausing for a moment to look at the cat family as a whole. Cats are consummate killers, their body shape perfect for the highly demanding art of capturing and killing live prey. They are sometimes referred to as hypercarnivores, because they need a much higher proportion of protein in their diet than almost any other mammal: domestic cats need 12 per cent protein (kittens require 18 per cent), while dogs can survive on just 4 per cent and thrive on a vegetarian diet, something that

Kike. Members of the order Carnivora are characterized by the distinctive carnassial or cheek teeth, designed like a pair of scissors to slice through the skin and flesh of their prey.

a cat would not be able to do (though our domestic moggy Geronimo obviously isn't aware of this, always happy to snack on avocado and broccoli). Cats match agility with power – their lithe bodies and flexible spines reflect this, and none more so than the cheetah, which uses a combination of long and rapid strides to reach speeds reportedly as fast as 114kph (68mph). To enable it to do this, it possesses enlarged lungs and heart to help maximize air intake.

As the cheetah races across the grasslands there are two phases in its stride when all four feet are off the ground: one when the front and back legs are extended and the other when the back legs reach forward and straddle the front legs in a fully flexed position, as can be seen from Angie's dramatic photo on the next page. The

suppleness of the spine and the easy rotation of the hips and shoulders allow for this impressive degree of extension and flexion, increasing both the length of the cheetah's stride and the speed at which it can run. Its stride as measured between two exactly similar points of contact by the same foot can be an incredible 23ft (7m).

The cheetah's feet are unusual in that the claws are blunt – except for the razor-sharp dewclaw on the wrists of the front paws (equivalent to our thumb) – helping it to gain purchase as it runs. The pads of its toes are different from those of a lion or leopard, being hard and more pointed to aid the sudden braking needed when a cheetah corners sharply, and the hind pad has tyre-like ridges to help it grip the ground. What you see when a cheetah runs

There are two points in a cheetah's stride when all four feet are off the ground. The total stride can measure an amazing 7m (23ft).

is a silky-smooth blend of flexibility, agility and breathtaking co-ordination.

All cats are digitigrade, which means that they walk on their toes, with the soft squidgy pads of their paws helping to distribute their weight to produce a fluid walking motion. Most have long, sinuous tails that measure at least one third of the length of their head and body; in the case of the arboreal margay, clouded leopard and marbled cat the tail is closer to half their length, making it easier for them to balance as they move through the trees. Snow leopards and mountain lions also have long tails, probably as an aid to moving about in mountainous terrain, while cheetahs use their long, tubular, rudder-like tails as a counterbalance when hunting fast-cornering prey.

A cat's skull is high domed with a foreshortened face (particularly in the case of the cheetah) and this, together with its powerful jaw muscles, increases the biting force of its long canines, which are designed as stabbing weapons for killing prey and for defence. The shortness of the face also means that the jaw has less space for teeth. Thus cats have fewer teeth than other carnivores – 28 or 30, compared to dogs' and bears' 42. In small cats the killing bite is usually aimed at the base of the skull or the neck. The tips of the canines are packed with nerve endings allowing them to 'feel' for the space between the neck vertebrae and place the bite accurately. The canines then act as a powerful wedge to pierce or break the spinal column.

The larger cats – including the cheetah – tend to use a throat bite, strangling or suffocating their prey, although the cheetah's relatively small canines, while effectively blocking the windpipe, do not generally pierce vital blood vessels. Between the canines in both top and bottom jaw is a row of small incisors used to hold, nibble and pluck flesh from a carcass. Most specialized of all are the carnassials or cheek teeth – the fourth premolar in the top jaw and the first molar in the bottom jaw – flattened, scissor-like teeth used to slice and shear through skin and flesh. It is remarkable how quickly a cheetah is able to open a gazelle or impala carcass using these powerful weapons.

Cats have the most highly developed binocular vision of all the carnivores. Their eyes are positioned well forward and high up on their skull, enabling them to judge distance accurately and pounce on their prey. They are equally adept at detecting prey on the darkest of nights and during the harsh light of midday, and are extremely large in relation to their body size. In fact a domestic cat's eyes are only slightly smaller than a human's, which, as Mel and Fiona Sunquist note in their excellent reference work *Wild Cats of the World*:

> *...may be partially responsible for their reputation for aloofness. Because its peripheral vision is so good, a resting cat needs to focus its eyes infrequently. The result is the cat's typical wide-eyed, staring-into-space look that some people find so unsettling.*

Interestingly, the cheetah's pupil is round, not diamond-shaped like those of lions and leopards; cheetahs have less need than their more nocturnal cousins to reduce the amount of light reaching the retina during the day.

It was long thought that cats did not perceive colour, partly because their eyes are so well adapted to seeing at night. The

Cheetahs have a razor-sharp dewclaw on their front paws, positioned on the inside of the wrist, to snag their prey.

retinas of all vertebrates, including humans, contain two types of light-sensitive cells: rods, which do not detect colour, and cones, which do. The cheetah's retina has an abundance of rods, but also a cluster of cones. Cats are thought to be able to see green, blue and possibly red, though having watched a leopard searching the ground for scraps of red meat that had fallen from its larder in a tree – and were highly visible to me – I am inclined to wonder. My observation certainly reinforces the speculation that cats see fewer colours than humans, and that those they do discern are far less saturated than the ones we see. Like birds of prey, cheetahs have a patch of highly light-sensitive cells on the retina known as the fovea, providing them with the most precise visual perception and enabling them to spot prey from as far away as 5km (3 miles).

Though cats lack the long, sensitive nose of members of the dog family, they do have a highly developed sense of smell. The deposition and location of scent are of great importance to all members of the cat family, who have scent glands situated around the anus, between their toes, on their cheeks and at the edge of their mouth. Spraying urine and depositing faeces in prominent positions is an important part of the way they communicate with one another, leaving complex chemical messages for the next cat who passes by and providing clues as to who left the scent, how long ago it was deposited and the sexual state of the owner.

The multitude of coat patterns exhibited by the different cat species is an indication of the large array of habitats in which they are found: cats come in every pattern imaginable from the uniformly tawny pelage of the lion to the bold stripes of the tiger and the spots of the cheetah and leopard. All are adaptations to helping the cat conceal itself. Those that live in desert conditions tend to be pale and sandy-coloured – the most northerly subspecies of cheetah, living on the fringes of the Sahara Desert, is very pale and rather indistinctly

spotted by comparison to those from East and southern Africa. Forest-dwelling cats tend to be darker and marked with spots or streaks that break up their outline, helping to conceal them in dappled light, whilst mountain-dwellers such as the puma often have light-coloured or greyish coats. These variations also help cats to recognize members of their own kind.

Because cheetahs lead a solitary and far-ranging existence they do not have an especially sophisticated 'language'. But they do have a number of distinctive and highly effective calls. The most common of these is 'yipping', a high-pitched contact call that mothers use to renew contact with their

cubs. Subadults make the same call when they become separated and males or females may yip when they want to make contact for breeding purposes. Cubs utter a higher version of this yip, which is normally referred to as 'chirping' and sounds very much like a plaintive bird call; they will sometimes do this even when they are with their mother, and in this context it may simply be a sign that they are feeling stressed. When a female is approached by a male or males, she may 'yelp', a shrill version of yipping used by a fearful animal who is eager to appease.

One of the most distinctive calls is heard when a mother 'churrs' (also known as

Honey strangling a Thomson's gazelle, whose front leg was broken when it was tripped and flipped through the air at high speed.

'stuttering' or 'stutter barking'). This is a deeper, more resonant, friendly sound. Kike would often use it when she was rounding up her cubs prior to moving. Strangers churr to express interest, uncertainty or appeasement, and the sound is heard frequently during interactions between males and females, and appears to function in the same way as 'prusten' or 'chuffling' in leopards and tigers – a series of soft, puffing, non-threatening sounds with which a mother calls her cubs or an adult lessens the tension and excitement of a meeting with another adult.

The cheetah's yip is said to carry for up to 2km (1 mile), but its inability to roar to announce its presence in a more forceful and far-carrying manner reflects the fact that female cheetahs – and some males – do not defend a territory, unlike lions and leopards, who advertise their presence to friend and enemy alike by uttering a powerful series of roars that in the case of the leopard can be heard for up to 3km (2 miles). The more social lion can be heard roaring from 5km (3 miles) or more, which helps to maintain contact with its own pride and to prevent members of other prides from encroaching.

The purpose of the cheetah's unique pattern of mascara-like tear marks running from the corner of each eye to the muzzle continues to puzzle biologists. Some have suggested that they might be similar in function to the black anti-glare paint employed by American footballers to stop the sun dazzling them. I think it is more likely that they accentuate facial expressions, an important consideration in social interactions with other cheetahs – and when trying to deter competitors from approaching, along with the growls and hisses that are an important part of a cheetah's defensive repertoire.

All cats tend to prey most heavily on a limited number of species that may vary from one area to another. Even leopards, the least specialized and most adaptable of the big cats, favour certain species in any given area, with impalas being one of the most commonly taken prey in savanna habitats and duikers and bushbucks in forested areas of both East and southern Africa. The distribution of the cheetah mirrors that of Thomson's gazelles, Grant's gazelles, impalas and gerenuks in East Africa, and impalas and springbok in southern Africa. Cheetahs kill on average once every one to three days – more often than lions and leopards, which have the luxury of being able to feed longer on their kills. The lions' size and the presence of companions enable them to defend their food from scavengers and feast until little is left. Leopards have the advantage of being able to drag their kill into a tree before the lions or hyenas can steal it, then feed on it for days at a time. The best a cheetah can hope for is to gorge itself before the vultures signal the presence of its kill to these larger competitors.

Cheetahs have always lost a portion of their prey to lions and hyenas. But they now face some far greater threats to their future – declining prey populations outside protected areas, loss of habitat to agriculture and livestock, poaching and illegal trade, and conflict with farmers. All five subspecies are listed by the Convention on International Trade in Endangered Species of Fauna and Flora (CITES) on Appendix 1 (animals that are 'threatened with extinction and are or may be affected by international commercial trade') and classified as Vulnerable or Endangered by the World Conservation Union (IUCN). A century ago there may have been as many as 100,000 cheetahs living throughout Africa and Asia. Today there are thought to be no more than 12,000–15,000 in Africa and, as we have seen, the tiniest remnant population in Asia. The situation is compounded by the cheetah's lack of genetic variability (we shall look further into this in Chapter 3) and the fact that many populations are fragmented and extremely small, with little chance of contact for breeding purposes. The cheetah may well be the ultimate leaned-down running machine, but it is poised on a knife edge, with man as its most dangerous adversary. Its fate lies in our hands.

Male cheetahs mark their territory by spraying urine mixed with anal-gland secretions against 'scent posts' such as trees. Scent is a very important means of communication for all cats.

Honey and her four five-month-old cubs feeding on a Thomson's gazelle. Cheetahs feed
quickly to lessen the risk of lions, hyenas or vultures stealing their kill.

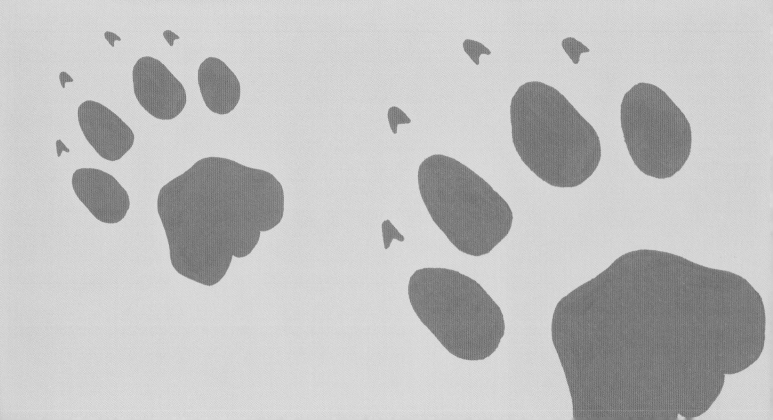

The Serengeti Cheetah

I saw my first wild cheetahs in the 1970s near the Gol Kopjes, a stunningly beautiful part of the Serengeti National Park in Tanzania, where the rock-hard backbone of Africa erupts from the land in the form of giant granite outcrops that tower above the plains. Some of the rocks around the centre of the park near Seronera date back to the time when the first stirrings of life appeared 3 billion years ago in the form of single-celled organisms. Not until much later – around 550 million years ago – during the Paleozoic or 'era of ancient life' did creatures with shells evolve, leaving signs of life in the form of fossils. Measured by those standards, the cheetah may be considered a relative newcomer to this ancient land.

The two cheetahs seemed to glide across the plains, their slim build and dainty stride giving them an air of vulnerability. As I watched them go I thought how superbly adapted they were to the vast open spaces, two tiny specks soon lost over the horizon as they continued their search for a wildebeest calf or a gazelle to add some temporary bulk to their slender frames.

There is no hint of menace about a cheetah, none of the thuggish heavyweight demeanour of the lion or the compact power of a leopard. A cheetah weighs as much as most leopards, but is taller with a more delicate bone structure, while the leopard is built like a middleweight boxer with powerful neck and sturdy limbs. One on one a cheetah would rather run for its life than face a leopard at close quarters, hardly surprising when you consider that given the chance a leopard will kill a cheetah and store it high in a tree to feast on at its leisure. Even when a cheetah is sprinting across the plains in pursuit of a gazelle you see speed harnessed to grace rather than brute strength, though the bulging upper leg and chest muscles that help power their explosive acceleration and reputedly allow them to reach speeds of 96kph (60mph) in two seconds would be the envy of an Olympic athlete.

Gol Kopjes, Serengeti. During the rainy season (November to May), more than a million wildebeest and 200,000 zebras gather to feast on the mineral-rich short-grass plains.

The end is normally as swift as the chase – the cheetah's long, slender forepaw reaches out and slaps or snags the back leg or flank of its prey with a razor-sharp dewclaw. In an instant the cat has its quarry by the throat, keeping well out of the way of the flailing hooves as it squeezes the life from its victim. But when it tackles larger prey such as a male impala or a wildebeest calf it may struggle to subdue it, with the quarry planting its feet wide, resisting attempts to topple it to the ground with the bull-like strength of the dying.

If its prey breaks free the cheetah risks serious injury on the ends of an impala's rapier-like horns or being kicked in the face by a bucking wildebeest calf. Once a prey animal is off its feet and pinned to the ground, it is much harder for it to rise again and resist the killing bite, even though a cheetah's canines are shorter and less dagger-like than those of a lion or leopard.

Having secured its meal the cheetah then drags it to cover, if there is any available, and lies panting before starting to eat – its body temperature will have skyrocketed to 40.5°C (105°F) and its respiration rate climbed from 60 to 150 beats per minute with the exertion.

So how does this sublime hunter survive among its larger competitors? The Serengeti, perhaps more than anywhere else in Africa, has helped to provide the answer to that question.

The Serengeti mirrors most people's idea of wild Africa. It certainly did mine, together with its northern extension in Kenya – the Masai Mara, where I was destined to make my home in years to come. The Serengeti is synonymous with wide vistas and blue skies that run for as far as the eye can see. It is a land of many faces; to the south lie the short-grass plains that spill over into the Ngorongoro Conservation Area (NCA), home during the rainy season to the wildebeest nation – all one and a half million of them. It is here that the cow wildebeest give birth, an annual spectacle of nearly half a million buff-coloured calves that provide a feast for all the larger predators – lions, leopards, hyenas, wild dogs and cheetahs. In an effort to safeguard against this, the calves are on their feet within five minutes, wobbling after their mothers as they take their first tentative steps on a life-long migration that in the course of each year will see them trek more than 3,000km (almost 2,000 miles).

Kopjes – Afrikaans for 'rock heads' – are ancient granite outcrops, providing shelter on the open plains for lions, leopards and even cheetahs at times.

This circuitous journey finds them spread like dark treacle across the treeless plains during the wet season that lasts from November until the end of May. Then onwards they hurry, over hillsides and through rivers as they search for water and fresh grazing during the dry season. They venture as far north as the Mara, where up to 600,000 wildebeest congregate at times, waiting for the onset of the short rains that normally begin in mid-October, signalling the start of their journey south again. By early December the herds are back on the short-grass plains, where the first calves appear in January. The birth season continues until March, with a peak in February, swamping the predators with a tide of young animals, ensuring that the majority survive.

In many ways the Serengeti and the NCA, which adjoins it to the east, are ideal places to study cheetahs. The Serengeti alone is 14,763km² (5,700sq. miles) in area and in conjunction with its neighbour provides a huge array of habitats, ranging from dry open plains and savanna woodlands to broken acacia country and rocky outcrops like the kopjes. It was the easy viewing out on the treeless plains that made the Serengeti such a joy for wildlife pioneering filmmakers such as Hugo van Lawick and Alan and Joan Root, who featured these elegant cats in a number of films, reinforcing the impression that the Serengeti was quintessential cheetah country, just as it appeared to be perfect for wild dogs.

We now know that such open terrain has its disadvantages, and may not necessarily be optimum habitat for either cheetahs or dogs. As scientists began to study these species in other parts of Africa, it became apparent that the seasonal distribution of prey – cheetahs and wild dogs hunt primarily Thomson's gazelles and wildebeest calves when they are grazing the plains during the rainy season – meant that these

Wildebeest calves gain their feet within five minutes of birth – faster than any other ungulate – and stay close to their mother throughout their first year.

predators must travel large distances over the course of a year to find sufficient food for themselves and their young. This prevents them reaching the densities seen in more wooded areas that provide adequate prey all year round. Both species are at the bottom of the predator hierarchy and suffer considerable competition from lions and spotted hyenas; and each has adopted its own very different strategies to cope with raising young under such taxing circumstances.

Wild dogs are the most social of all the large predators and the life of a pack is centred around a dominant pair – the alpha male and female – who monopolize breeding. Each year the alpha female selects a den site, usually an abandoned aardvark or warthog burrow, where she gives birth to an average of ten puppies (though up to 19 have been recorded) after a gestation period of ten weeks.

Finding sufficient food is the priority for any animal with young, and wild dogs breed seasonally throughout their range. In the Serengeti, packs living on the short-grass plains time the birth of their puppies to coincide with the rainy season, when the wildebeest and gazelles are calving – a wildebeest calf is the ideal size of prey for a pack of dogs. Some 200km (120 miles) further north in the Mara, wild dogs living in and around the reserve have their puppies during the dry season, with a peak in births between June and August, by which time the wildebeest and their calves have migrated to this area, providing a welcome addition to the gazelles, impalas and topis that sustain the dogs for the rest of the year. All the pack members, including the previous year's puppies, help to feed their younger relatives, and once the pups are three months old they are strong enough to leave the safety of their underground sanctuary and follow the adults, allowing the pack to resume its wanderings.

Cheetahs breed at any time of the year, though in the Serengeti they are more likely to conceive successfully in the wet season, possibly because of the increase in the number of gazelle fawns. Fawns are easy to catch, and are the preferred prey of young cheetahs and of adult females. Another factor that may be responsible for this seasonal peak is that a female who loses her cubs in the dry season takes longer to conceive again than one whose cubs die in the wet season. Better nutrition seems to be the most likely reason for this, though studies on domestic cats have shown that the greatest nutritional demand on a pregnant female is in the last stage of pregnancy, when resorption is least likely. Oestrus in some species is triggered by day length, but this varies little in equatorial climes, so would not be a factor in the Serengeti. Studies on cheetahs in other parts of Africa may be able to shed light on whether or not an abundant and readily available supply of food provides a stimulus for seasonal breeding. Certainly leopards in the Mara appear to give birth more commonly during the long dry season of July to October and at the beginning of the rainy season, when the young of their commonest prey, the impala, and of a number of other species such as warthogs and topis, are most abundant. Research on lions in the Serengeti points to an increase in reproductive activity when the wildebeest

migration is in residence and lionesses are in peak condition, and cubs born at this time are more likely to be well nourished.

There is no doubt that the Serengeti's short-grass plains are an ideal location for a cheetah during the rainy season. Hundreds of thousands of gazelles dazzle the eye in the sharp morning light as they swarm across the landscape, the brilliant whiteness of their bellies shimmering like shoals of fish as they race this way and that when disturbed by a hunting predator. But when the throngs of gazelles, wildebeest and zebras turn their backs on the drying plains and migrate further north and west at the beginning of the dry season, the predators

Wild dog puppies spend their first three months at an underground den – usually an abandoned aardvark burrow or hyena den.

Wild dog chasing wildebeest across the Serengeti plains. Dogs synchronize the birth of their puppies to the abundance of food represented by the migration of wildebeest and gazelles.

must follow, and many of the cheetahs move to the woodland edge around Seronera, where the Thomson's gazelles congregate. The home range – the place where an animal lives and which it patrols on a regular basis – of both cheetahs and wild dogs reflects these movements. The packs of dogs that I watched on the Serengeti plains in the mid-1980s occupied ranges of about 1,000–2,000km² (400–800sq. miles), and female cheetahs

Thomson's gazelle cleaning her fawn. A cheetah's success rate is almost 100 per cent when hunting young Tommies.

here have ranges that average 800km² (300sq. miles). But in the Mara the ranges are much smaller: the wild dogs range over about half the area covered by the plains-dwelling packs, and cheetah females occupy ranges of about 80–100km² (30–40sq. miles), with most males ranging over somewhat smaller areas. This marked difference is due to the abundance and variety of prey in the woodland areas of the Mara, which enjoy double the rainfall of the southern Serengeti and receive some rain in every month of the year. In the Serengeti, when the rains stop at the end of May, the grass withers and the alkaline pools dry up, and it is only dry-country species such as the ostrich and fringe-eared oryx that can eke out a living.

When people first started to study cheetahs in the wild they were puzzled. Cheetahs didn't seem to be as solitary as most members of the cat family, but neither were they as social as lions. It was difficult to work out whether they were territorial – like most cats – or simply migrated in pursuit of their prey, as seemed to be the

case in the Serengeti. Early reports described every possible combination – solitary females and solitary males, groups of adult males and aggregations of up to six seemingly adult cheetahs of both sexes; occasionally one or more adult males were seen in the company of a female and her cubs – a family of cheetahs no less. It was all very confusing.

In most cats – certainly big cats such as tigers, leopards and jaguars – adult males and adult females defend separate territories which they demarcate by laying down scent, by roaring and by their physical presence. When necessary, a territory holder will actively defend its home range against any other breeding adult who tries to settle there. This system of land tenure helps to space individuals within a population, reducing competition for food and ensuring (insofar as this is possible) that there is sufficient prey to sustain everyone all year round. One would normally expect an area where prey was plentiful to support a higher density of predators.

A bachelor herd of Thomson's gazelles on the Serengeti's short-grass plains. Adult male gazelles leave the bachelor herds to stake out a territory.

We now know that female cheetahs are solitary – so too are some male cheetahs, although male littermates stay together as adults. Lone males – generally those who have no surviving brothers when the time comes for them to leave their mother – sometimes form a permanent association with one or more others as a way of increasing their chances of holding a territory, preferably in an area where there are plenty of females to breed with. Alternatively a male may roam as a nomad or floater, mating with as many females as he can and at the same time trying to avoid contact with coalitions of males who might attack and kill him. In the Serengeti a female's home range may contain three or four male territories, and she may mate with any of these territorial males – or with a floater passing through, for that matter. Mixed-sex groups of large cheetahs are more often than not littermates who have recently left their mother; these subadults remain together for up to six months until the females separate from their brothers around the time of their first oestrus. Such a group may also be a mother and cubs accompanied (usually briefly) by an adult male who is checking on the reproductive status of the female.

The American biologist George Schaller was one of the first people to study cheetahs in the Serengeti, at the same time as he conducted his pioneering project on lions in the park from 1966 to 1969. At that time little was known about these graceful cats, beyond the fact that they were the fastest thing on four legs, hunted mainly during the daytime and were capable of giving birth to large litters.

As Schaller explored the many moods of the Serengeti, by night as well as by day, he derived a quiet joy from his meetings with animal acquaintances on his daily rounds. There was Corky, the three-legged crocodile, George, the bull giraffe, and 'in the sparse shade of a whistling thorn, a cheetah female'. Schaller came to know that cheetah well, though he never gave her a

Very young cheetah cubs have a mantle of long silvery-grey hair running along their neck and back, helping to camouflage them.

name, commenting that 'her look of amber arrogance seemed to forbid such intimacy'. He watched as she struggled to raise the litter of young cubs she had hidden in a kopje – a somewhat risky course of action as lions and leopards often used the kopjes as both a resting place and a den. A month later the cheetah abandoned her lair and brought the three cubs into the open. From that time onwards the cubs had no fixed abode and followed their mother wherever she chose to hunt. One disappeared, but the other two – both females – survived.

Watching the tiny cubs during their first few months, Schaller pondered the reason for their long natal coat, a mantle of silvery-grey hair that stretches from the top of their head to the base of their tail and

might appear to make the young conspicuous and even more vulnerable to predation. The most obvious reason for these unusual markings is that they help to camouflage the cubs when they begin to move about with their mother, allowing them to blend more easily with the long stands of silvery grass. Some people have suggested that the coat makes cheetah cubs resemble the honey badger or ratel, as feisty an adversary as any predator is likely to meet, though the deterrent effect of such a guise is questionable, given that lions, hyenas and leopards show no hesitation in killing young cheetahs. By the time the cubs are three to four months old the long hair has gone, except for a short ruff on the back of the neck that male cheetahs retain

Honey licking blood from the face of one of her cubs. Cheetahs are not as tactile as the social lions, though adult males do groom each other, helping to reinforce social bonds.

in shortened form throughout their life. At this age cheetah cubs are able to run fast enough to outpace most predators.

Schaller's female avoided contact with other cheetahs, even though she shared an area used by a number of adult females without any sign of friction. She proved to be a good mother, calling the cubs whenever they fell behind, using a high-pitched, bird-like chirrup followed by a churring sound, and licking the cubs after a meal to clean the blood from their faces. All of them purred contentedly during these activities, yet Schaller noted that they lacked the intense and uninhibited desire to touch one another that characterizes lions.

Finding food seemed to be the cheetah mother's primary concern, and for 26 consecutive days late one dry season either Schaller, his wife Kay or friends waited to see her hunt. Having spent every waking hour for six weeks with Kike and her three cubs last summer, Angie and I know just what that entails, cocooned in your vehicle, the sun beating down, not a tree in sight, waiting for the moment when the cheetah will rise from its resting place to seek prey.

The Serengeti female killed 24 gazelles and one hare during those 26 days. Only about half her chases after adult gazelles were successful, but when her target was a fawn she almost invariably caught it. With their slim build and relatively weak jaws, cheetahs – particularly females – tend to select prey of around their own weight or smaller, which limits them to creatures of a maximum of 60kg (130lb) and makes gazelles, impalas and reedbucks their most popular prey. Male cheetahs are bigger and stronger than females, and on average 10 per cent heavier, which allows them to take larger prey. I once saw three male cheetahs at the edge of Musiara Marsh, feeding on a freshly killed female zebra who might have weighed 220kg (485lb), and there are a number of records of males in the Serengeti killing both yearling and adult wildebeest, though they battle to pull such large creatures to the ground and strangle them. Small, vulnerable prey – young gazelles, impalas and hares – are obvious targets, as are the sick or injured. In fact any animal of the right size that makes itself vulnerable, by seeking cover or putting its head down to feed, unwittingly selects itself.

But even when a cheetah has killed, there is always the risk that it will lose its meal to a larger predator, and of the 25 kills made by the female that Schaller watched three were commandeered by lions or hyenas – 12 per cent. A determined mob of vultures may also gather in sufficient numbers to drive a cheetah from its kill before it has gorged itself. Hardly surprisingly, therefore, cheetahs feed quickly and nervously, constantly sitting up and glancing around, ever watchful for the arrival of lions or hyenas, who may be alerted to the kill by the distress calls of the victim or the spiral of vultures marking the place. With fewer lions living out on the plains than in the woodlands, cheetahs in open country suffer less competition from them, but have to contend with a high density of spotted hyenas – there are more than 5,000 on the Serengeti plains and around 7,500 in the park as a whole.

The cheetah remained in an area of about 60 km² (23sq. miles) near Seronera

Two of Honey's cubs grooming after a large meal.

Cheetahs give birth to larger litters than lions or leopards – on average four, though up to six is not unusual and one instance of ten cubs has been recorded in Nairobi National Park.

Newborn cheetahs weigh only 250–400gm (9–14oz), less than a third of the weight of a lion cub. This small size reduces stress on a pregnant female who must hunt for herself.

for five months, then vanished. Schaller was the first person to discover that most of the Serengeti's cheetahs migrate with the gazelles as they head back to the eastern plains with the arrival of the rains. For months not a single cheetah visited his study area, and the female didn't return until June, by which time the rainy season had drawn to a close. By now the two cubs were almost as large as she was, though somewhat lighter in build and with the typical adolescent ruff. A few months later,

when the youngsters were 15 months old, mother and cubs split up. Kay Schaller saw the family together for the last time one evening; then by the next afternoon they had gone their separate ways.

The manner of their parting surprised Schaller. There was no warning, no gradual weakening of the bond, such as you see with lions or leopards. Leopard cubs in particular are often left on their own, sometimes for days, while their mother goes off hunting. They gradually start taking small prey for themselves and are very independent in their mien. However, subadult leopards who have parted from their mother do sometimes meet up with her again and may be permitted to feed on her kills; they still share her territory, which is small by comparison to a cheetah's home range and makes it possible for them to track their mother down. Even when a female leopard is fully grown, she and her mother may share overlapping territories and tolerate each other's presence, though

they generally avoid each other – as do cheetahs. Lions, being social, have taken this process a stage further, with young lionesses often staying on as adults as part of the core of the pride, and the territory being passed on through the female line over many generations.

Jim Cavanaugh, who for many years has followed the lions and cheetahs in Nairobi National Park, experienced the same surprise as Schaller when he saw Nanette, the cheetah female he had been watching, literally turn on her five cubs when they were 15½ months old and chase them away.

The mother cheetah and the adolescents Schaller was watching hunted in the same area and occasionally saw one another at a distance, but they acted like strangers. Unable to hunt as efficiently as adults at this stage in their life, the two sisters grew lean, but they survived and in December disappeared again, no doubt following the gazelles as they migrated back to the plains with the onset of the rains.

When not tracking lions, Schaller continued to monitor the cheetahs. In February the next year he found one of the sisters, now 19 months old, near the hauntingly beautiful Barafu Kopjes, some 40km (25 miles) east of Seronera. By late April the young female was back at Seronera, and the following month her sister re-appeared. A few weeks later their mother arrived in the area, accompanied by three new cubs, though one was sickly and soon disappeared. Schaller decided to try to keep track of the young female, who gave birth for the first time in July at the age of two years.

Cheetah cubs are born after a gestation period of 90–95 days. When a female is near the end of her pregnancy she must find somewhere secluded to give birth – this may be deep in the thick vegetation of a marsh, in a rocky outcrop, tucked away among a tangle of bushes along a lugga or merely buried in a patch of long grass moulded by the contours of the mother's body. Ronald McLaughlin, who studied cheetahs in Nairobi Park in the late 1960s, found that the females there chose areas of long grass for their dens.

Life in a cheetah den is shrouded in mystery, and it is almost impossible to observe details of the cubs' development during the first few weeks without disturbing the mother and prompting her to move. Cubs are born with their eyes tightly closed and they weigh just 250-400gm (9–14oz), no more than a rat; the small size of the foetuses doubtless helps reduce stress on a pregnant female who must hunt for herself – among the social lions, cubs can weigh up to 1.5kg (3lb) at birth. According to zoo records, cheetah cubs are born at intervals of 20–30 minutes, with the mother breaking each foetal membrane with her teeth and consuming the placenta.

Joy Adamson, who wrote the best-selling book *Born Free* about a lioness called Elsa whom she and her game-warden husband George eventually returned to the wild, also released a captive-raised cheetah named Pippa into a game sanctuary in Kenya, where she mated successfully with a wild male. Pippa's first litter numbered three cubs and she subsequently produced three more litters, all of four cubs. She had 13 teats, though the norm is ten to twelve – two to three times a lioness's or leopard's four. The six cheetah litters Ronald McLaughlin observed in Nairobi Park numbered from three to six cubs with an average of 4.3. The cheetah's ability to produce larger litters seems to be an adaptation to the high mortality that cubs generally suffer.

Adamson recorded that whenever Pippa was about to give birth, she chose such thick bush for her den that it was virtually impossible to get anywhere near it or see into it. However, Joy was able to establish that newborn cubs could crawl to their mother's teats, stand by the age of nine days and walk unsteadily by two weeks, though they often fell down. Their eyes normally open at some point during the second week, when they around ten or eleven days old.

Pippa moved her second litter 21 times in the first six weeks, and her fourth 14 times, usually to a bush up to 180m (200yd) away. (Hyenas are known to have accounted for one of her other two litters, and the remaining one was also taken by predators.) In McLaughlin's study, cubs were moved far less than this, on average three times in the first six weeks. Moving cubs helps to prevent a build-up of scent that might attract unwelcome attention from predators, so the frequency of movement no doubt depends to a degree on the amount of disturbance to which the mother is subjected – cheetahs are known to abandon litters in very difficult circumstances. Cubs are carried by the scruff of the neck or sometimes by the leg or body in the rather haphazard manner that I have seen wild dog mothers use when transporting young puppies to a new den. By the time cheetah cubs are three weeks old their teeth have begun to appear and they can walk. By four weeks they have become difficult to carry, and at six weeks are highly mobile and may even have been led to their first kill.

Generally cheetah cubs are fully weaned by the time they are three months old – younger than lions or leopards, who may continue to suckle for a month or two longer than this. Leopard mothers often bring a small kill back to their cubs rather than risk exposing them to the danger of following her, and being social a lioness has the added benefit of having her pride mates there to help ward off the dangers posed by other predators. A mother cheetah, on the other hand, has no choice but to mobilize her cubs as soon as possible, allowing her to range more widely in search of food. But the dangers facing the cubs are daunting.

After Schaller's study ended, the mission of finding out more about the Serengeti cheetahs was taken up by George and Lorie Frame. From the mid-1970s they spent the best part of five years following cheetahs and wild dogs and subsequently published their findings in scientific journals and in a most readable book entitled *Swift and Enduring*. The Frames' first task was to find the best way of identifying the cheetahs they saw. Lion researchers use the pattern of whisker spots as a fingerprint – each lion retains its unique muzzle print throughout its life. Although a cheetah's whisker spots are not as easily distinguishable as this, its spots are.

The Frames gradually built up an identification file of photographs, noting the position of the spots on the face, chest, legs and tail of each individual. They soon found that every spot on every cheetah was uniquely positioned and that tail markings showed a greater similarity among littermates. By the end of their study they had 442 cheetahs on file. Today researchers use a computer program that matches new photographs with the existing file, making the process of identification far less time-consuming.

Since Schaller's day, subsequent observations have shown that the abrupt transition from dependence to full independence is the norm for cheetahs, though very occasionally a mother and her subadult offspring will reunite briefly. Simon King filmed such a reunion while following Amber and three large cubs in 1998. We had been expecting the family to split up at any moment, and sure enough one day Simon found that mother and youngsters had gone their separate ways. Not long after this the three cubs chanced upon their mother and stalked towards her in a manner reminiscent of the way male cheetahs approach females. They adopted an intimidating stance and proceeded with a measured stride, heads held low, eyes unblinking. Amber responded submissively, attempting to slink away while at the same time uttering high-pitched yelps with her mouth open in a submissive 'fear face'. No blows were exchanged, and suddenly the tension evaporated; the cubs gambolled after their mother as she bounded away. Then they greeted one another in what could only be described as a joyful reunion. But the die was cast; the young cheetahs were ready to move on, and by the following morning the family had parted company once more and were never seen together again. A few months later Amber gave birth to a new litter of cubs.

Amber's three cubs, aged around 16 months, with the female on the right. Note the difference in size between males and females.

Kike carrying a week-old cub to a new den. A cheetah mother regularly moves her cubs during the first few weeks, probably in an effort to prevent detection by predators.

The primary focus of the Frames' work was to evaluate the conservation status of cheetahs in the Serengeti ecosystem. It was evident that cheetahs throughout Africa existed in far lower numbers than leopards or lions. This could no longer be explained by dint of the cheetah being considered an atypical and specialized cat. Schaller had already noted that cheetahs were capable of surviving well enough in places like the Serengeti, despite the odds seemingly being

stacked against them with so many larger predators to compete with. He had estimated that there were 2,000 lions, perhaps 900 leopards and 200–250 cheetahs in the Serengeti, and nobody doubted that there were more spotted hyenas than all the cats added together. The Frames were now in a position to provide a more accurate estimate of cheetah numbers, and to try to answer some of the other questions that Schaller's work had raised. For instance, were cheetahs rare by comparison to the other cats due to competition for food and space, or were numbers declining for other reasons? Whatever the answer, observers felt that cub survival had deteriorated since Schaller's study ten years earlier.

This was the kind of research of which Myles Turner, the Warden of the Serengeti from 1956 to 1972, would have approved. He had questioned the need for studies based simply on behaviour when money was in such short supply in the war he was waging against poachers. Turner wanted answers to questions that had a bearing on park management. Only by knowing how many cheetahs there were in Serengeti and

whether or not their numbers were declining – and if so why – could anyone make decisions on how to conserve them.

Of immediate concern was to try to determine how many cubs cheetahs were giving birth to and the exact reasons for their poor survival rate. Even though Schaller had estimated that up to half of all cheetah cubs disappeared by the time they were three months old, in the early 1970s it was not uncommon to see a mother cheetah with five or even six cubs. In Nairobi Park Jim Cavanaugh has regularly seen cheetahs with five or six cubs, and Nanette, the cheetah he got to know best, produced litters of seven, eight, six, six and five between 1993 and 1998. Of the 21 cubs in her first three litters, she managed to raise 13 (62 per cent) to adulthood. This is an astonishing feat when you consider that in the Serengeti – on the plains at least – most females rear fewer than two cubs to independence in an average lifespan of seven years. Nanette's daughter Isquierda broke all previous records when she was seen with ten three-month-old cubs in April 1998, though she appears to have abandoned them a month later, presumably

Half-Tail carrying a warthog piglet back to where she has left her cubs safely hidden – typical behaviour for a mother leopard when her cubs first start eating meat at six to eight weeks.

Schaller's study helped lay the foundation for more intensive research on cheetahs. He estimated that there were 200–250 of these enigmatic cats in the Serengeti, and that such low densities were typical of most other parks and reserves. Despite cub mortality being about 50 per cent, Schaller felt that cheetahs were quite prolific and many survived to adulthood. Yet something didn't quite add up. His thoughts and findings offered a challenge to the next generation of researchers who came to study cheetahs in the Serengeti:

'They have reached a peak of evolutionary efficiency in their hunting. Then why are they so sparse, why is the species balanced so delicately between security and extinction? Their refusal to breed in captivity puzzles me too. Thousands of cheetahs have been kept in zoos and by Eastern potentates who trained them to hunt antelope, yet only about a dozen births have been recorded. Looking into their haunting eyes, I am aware that the cheetah remains an enigma.'

daunted by the effort of feeding and nurturing such a large family. Cavanaugh is adamant that this huge litter was not a case of orphans from a second litter being 'adopted', and attributes the ability of cheetah females in Nairobi Park to raise large litters to the relatively low lion and hyena populations.

The largest litter that the Frames observed was six, with an average of four when cubs were still in the den. They found that by the time cheetah cubs were three months old and following their mother, often only two or three had survived, with many of the losses presumably due to their inability to outrun predators. In fact it is a miracle that any cubs survive at all, as they are preyed on by jackals and the smaller cats as well as by all the larger predators. The photographer Dave Richards once witnessed a secretary bird swooping down and killing a week-old cheetah cub in the Mara when vehicles disturbed its mother while she was moving her litter. The giant bird lashed out at the defenceless cub with its foot, stomping it to death as it would a grass rat. The Frames estimated that 70 per cent of cheetah cubs failed to survive to adulthood – the majority dying in the first three months – and often entire litters were lost.

The Frames were still working in the Serengeti when Tanzania decided to close its border with Kenya in 1977, a decision that was to have major repercussions for tourism and wildlife conservation in both countries. Tanzania had become increasingly frustrated by Kenya's domination of its tourist industry, with Nairobi touted as the safari capital of the world. Visitors to Tanzania's spectacular wilderness areas – the Serengeti, Ngorongoro Crater, Lake Manyara and, in the south of the country, the great Selous Game Reserve and Ruaha National Park – often arrived in Kenya-registered vehicles accompanied by Kenya-based safari guides. So although tourists flocked to Tanzania, most of the revenue remained in Kenya. Socialism and capitalism were on a collision course, and inevitably the East African Community collapsed.

With the border closed and revenue from tourism at an all-time low, Tanzania's parks struggled to support themselves – and to stem the rise in poaching that soon ensued. Work at the Serengeti Research Institute, which for so many years had attracted scientists from all over the world, began to grind to a halt. Fuel, vehicle spares and food supplies were hard to come by. But with the help of people like Barbie Allen in Nairobi, who forwarded mail and purchased spares, the Serengeti lion and cheetah projects somehow managed to keep scientists in the field throughout these difficult times, providing an unrivalled database on Africa's large predatory cats. Meanwhile, I had just arrived in the Mara, ready to capitalize on the chance to get to know the lions, leopards and cheetahs on a more personal basis.

Zawadi's three-month-old cubs in early 2000. Safi, on the right, looks wary, as she has continued to do as an adult. Her more outgoing brother was killed by lions at six months.

Life in the Den

Once the Kenya–Tanzania border reopened in 1983, I was free to visit the Serengeti again, and between 1986 and 1988 I spent many months there collecting material for books on the wildebeest migration and wild dogs. There were times when I lived in my car, rising before dawn each morning and bedding down in the back once it was dark, mirroring the lives of the animals I was following. I studied packs of dogs roaming the vastness of the southern plains and the woodland thickets of the Western Corridor. Occasionally I would chance upon a cheetah with small cubs out on the plains or stalking through the acacia woodlands, and stop to watch them for a while. I would wait to see if the mother might kill, and if she was successful watch as the family fed hurriedly in case a lion or hyena happened along. On one occasion a huge male lion did just that, chasing the family away and robbing them of a fresh Grant's gazelle kill, a sizeable meal. The lion was an outcast from his pride, ousted by a new generation of younger, fitter males, forced now to survive as best he could on the plains among the other nomads.

Not uncommonly, the next time I saw the family, one or more of the cubs would have disappeared, and all of us working in the Serengeti were beginning to wonder what was happening. The recent publication of Dr Stephen O'Brien's research into the genetics of the African cheetah population had turned the debate over their wellbeing into headline news.

In 1981, the director of the National Zoological Gardens of South Africa (NZGSA) invited representatives of the American National Zoological Park (ANZS), under the leadership of Stephen O'Brien of the American Cancer Foundation, to try to discover why it was so difficult to breed cheetahs in captivity. The NZGSA had founded a cheetah-breeding programme at the De Wilt Cheetah Breeding and Research Centre near Pretoria in 1971. It housed 80 cheetahs from two distinct

regions of southern Africa – Namibia and the northern region of what was then Transvaal Province in South Africa, areas which are separated by 1,500km (900 miles) of the mighty Kalahari Desert. Even though the centre had managed to breed cheetahs, the authorities were perplexed by the cats' seemingly poor fertility and high rate of infant mortality – 37 per cent. As we have seen, cheetahs have proved difficult to breed since the days of the Mogul emperors; the first cubs born in a zoo were in Philadelphia as recently as 1956, and since then only a small number of breeding programmes have been successful (with Ann van Dyk, director and founder of De Wilt, leading the way, having bred over 600 cubs since the centre's inception).

Perhaps even more worrying was that only 10–15 per cent of wild-caught adult cheetahs had reproduced in captivity. This was partly due to unsuccessful mating attempts, but even when mating was successful the cheetahs had a low conception rate compared with other zoo-bred species. So what ailed them?

When O'Brien and his associates published their findings, it had a huge impact in the field of conservation biology. I received a copy of their monograph published in *Scientific American* with the headline 'Can the cheetah survive?' I remember sitting in my car in the middle of the Serengeti, surrounded by a pack of wild dogs in peak condition, and suddenly feeling horribly depressed. The paper stated that the cheetah was in genetic peril and in a race for survival. Apparently an ancient population bottleneck had resulted in genetic uniformity, making the species

Cheetah cubs can crawl at birth, walk unsteadily at three weeks and begin to follow their mother at seven to eight weeks. Even tiny cubs will hiss and spit if feeling threatened.

vulnerable to ecological change – the more diversity a species has, the more likely it is that at least some individuals will survive changed circumstances. The scientists' findings showed that cheetahs from as far apart as East and southern Africa – populations isolated by thousands of kilometres – were as similar to one another as 20 generations of deliberately inbred livestock or laboratory mice. Was this indeed the end of the road for the cheetah?

I met O'Brien in the Mara in the late 1980s. We were being filmed for an American wildlife documentary on big cats, with me as the resident naturalist. O'Brien had teamed up with Dr Pieter Kat from the genetics section of the National Museum in Nairobi to help formulate a disease-management plan for areas where the cheetah was thought to be especially vulnerable. O'Brien and his co-workers were instrumental in initiating the National Cheetah Research Master Plan (NCRMP), co-ordinating detailed studies in the medical, reproductive and genetic health of free-living and captive cheetahs, and an International Cheetah Studbook was already in place to record births, deaths, sires and dams of all cheetahs in captivity. If the cheetah was indeed imperilled, then

Four seven-month-old cubs playing. Cubs that have survived to this age have a good chance of making it to adulthood.

perhaps there was some way that man could help.

One of the experiments O'Brien and his associates performed to test just how closely related the two groups of southern African cheetahs at De Wilt were, was to exchange skin grafts between members of each group. In unrelated animals the survival time for skin grafts averages ten to twelve days. But on this occasion all the grafts were accepted, though some were later slowly rejected. Several grafts persisted for at least 78 days, by which time they appeared to blend in with the recipient's own skin. This startling result indicated that the cheetahs' immune systems did not recognize the tissue as being from another

animal, and therefore failed to produce an immune reaction. Bear in mind that this was at a time when the medical profession was struggling with the problem of tissue rejection in organ transplants in humans. Finding a tissue match with a member of a person's immediate family was no guarantee that the organ would not be rejected, even with the help of potent anti-rejection drugs. Yet regardless of which population of cheetahs was tested and how isolated they were from one another, the results were the same.

Like the best forensic sleuths, O'Brien speculated on how this situation might have arisen. As we have seen, roughly 20,000 years ago cheetahs ranged around the world, but about 10,000 years ago, as the last great ice age drew to a close, dramatic changes in climate caused 75 per cent of mammals (including mammoths, mastodons, giant sloths and the sabre-toothed cats) to vanish from Europe and North America. Only small populations of cheetahs in Asia and Africa survived, and all the cheetahs now living are descended from this handful of individuals. At one stage scientists thought it possible that only a single pregnant female had survived the holocaust, but this idea has since been dismissed.

Mammals have a natural tendency to avoid incest due to the damaging genetic consequences of inbreeding, but under these circumstances cheetahs would have had no alternative but to breed with close

Honey's cubs, aged five months. Play such as this helps to exercise young muscles and refine innate hunting abilities such as stalking, pouncing and biting.

relatives. Consequently all the cheetahs alive today share 99 per cent of the same genes, which is equivalent to having only 1–10 per cent of the genetic difference shown by members of other cat species such as lions and leopards. It is known that a population that is reduced to as few as seven individuals can still retain about 95 per cent of its original genetic variation, but only if the survivors expand their numbers quickly. Slow expansion in a small population increases the likelihood that different gene types will disappear, and O'Brien felt that on one or more occasions in the past the cheetah population had dropped to a very few individuals, 'escaping extinction by a whisker', and that possibly the survivors never managed to expand their numbers rapidly enough to avoid loss of genetic variety.

The reasons for such declines, apart from climatic catastrophe such as an ice age, range from viral or bacterial plagues to destruction of habitat or outright killing by humans. As we have seen, the cheetah was not alone in succumbing to whatever misfortune prompted its numbers to dwindle so dramatically. Numerous ungulate species died off at the end of the Pleistocene, due perhaps to changes in vegetation, which in turn would have affected the predators. Both the North American lion and the California sabre-tooth *Smilodon* became extinct, as did lions and leopards over much of Eurasia, and the last of the North American cheetahs *Miracinonyx* disappeared. We can only guess at what role our ancestors' rapid rise to power played in all this. O'Brien later concluded that persecution by humans around a hundred years ago may have caused a second bottleneck that resulted in the southern African population becoming even more compromised than its East African relatives.

Whether this is true or not, man's impact has certainly been detrimental to all the African predators, not just the cheetahs. When Europeans came to Africa they looked at the land with the eyes of farmers and hunters, seeing the wilderness as something to be tamed and fenced off. There was ivory to be exploited, skins to be traded, predators to be eradicated, land to be cleared to make way for cattle and crops. In South Africa vast numbers of animals were killed in order to feed the gangs of men working on the railway linking the goldfields with the coast. In 1884 President Paul Kruger demanded that some kind of sanctuary be created to protect the wild animals, but his suggestion fell on deaf ears. Before long the great herds of springboks and hartebeest had gone, and so had many of the predators.

In 1898 the South African House of Assembly finally passed the motion establishing the 4,600km^2 (1800sq. miles) Sabi Game Reserve (it would later become Kruger National Park). A year later the Boer War broke out. It lasted for four long years, with soldiers from both sides slaughtering huge numbers of animals. Even when peace was restored, predators continued to be seen as vermin – anti-predator sentiments even extended to the management of the Sabi Reserve, despite the fact that the park's inception had been inspired by the ideal of preserving wildlife within its borders and eliminating the influence of man. Because such huge numbers of animals had been shot for meat, it was decided to cull predators to give the prey species a chance to recover; it was even standard practice to control carnivorous reptiles and birds of prey. The aim was supposedly to reduce the impact of predators – not to eradicate them, as it was on settled areas where carnivores were shot on sight. The settlers had little time for game reserves and saw them as a sanctuary for animals which were a threat to their livestock. In fact they clamoured for even more culling.

Fortunately the first warden of Sabi, James Stevenson-Hamilton, had a more enlightened view of game management than many of his contemporaries. He realized that there existed a natural balance between predator and prey, and that predators helped to keep prey populations healthy by killing old and weak animals. Nevertheless, the minimum numbers of predators that Stevenson-Hamilton and his staff killed between 1903 and 1927 make sobering reading: they accounted for 1,272 lions, 660 leopards, 269 cheetahs, 521 spotted and brown hyenas, and 1,142 wild dogs. Little wonder that the cheetah soon found itself endangered all over again, and

In the 1980s, 60,000 elephants were being killed in Africa each year, leading to a 50 per cent decline in the population. Trade in ivory was banned in 1989.

Marsh lioness grooming a cub. Lionesses generally remain in their natal pride, though if there are too many in a pride, young females must leave and try to establish themselves elsewhere.

as human populations increase still further, the demand for land can only grow with it, compounding the problems. In fact, conflict with livestock owners is now the most serious threat facing Africa's big cats outside protected areas.

Though nobody could be certain of the significance of O'Brien's findings, it seemed highly likely that during times of ecological and environmental change such as temperature shifts, drought, glaciation or spates of epidemic disease the cheetah would be at a disadvantage. This put it in the same category as other genetically impoverished species such as the California sea otter and elephant seal, which have very little variability among their immune systems and may therefore be at greater

risk of decimation by a new virus or other disease. In a normal outbred population (such as most human societies), some individuals will cope better than others during an outbreak of an infectious disease. For example, when a flu epidemic sweeps through a region, certain individuals suffer less – or not at all – because their immune system fights off the virus more efficiently than other people's. In the case of the northern elephant seal at least there was a happy ending. A hundred years ago only about 20 remained in the wild, but with the advent of protective legislation the population has gradually recovered and now numbers tens of thousands.

Just how difficult it was for the cheetah to deal with a potentially lethal disease – in

captivity at least – became evident when an outbreak of feline infectious peritonitis (FIP) struck a captive breeding centre in Oregon in 1982. This virus has a low mortality rate in the genetically diverse domestic cat (no more than 10 per cent), but it ended up killing 50 per cent of the cheetahs, the most extreme response to FIP reported for any species. Since then similarly lethal outbreaks among captive cheetahs have been reported from breeding centres in Ireland, Canada and Namibia. On the other hand, ten African lions in the Oregon compound showed no signs of infection, and the possibility that the outbreak had been caused by a particularly virulent form of FIP was discounted when domestic cats inoculated with the same virus failed to become infected. This seemed to confirm that the cheetahs were hardest hit because of their vulnerability rather than because of any particular virulence in this strain of the disease.

Fortunately wild cheetahs do not seem to be very prone to disease, and vaccine trials on captive cheetahs have shown that they are well equipped to deal with a variety of pathogens. However, the threat to all wild species from diseases spread by domestic stock is well documented. In 1994 the Serengeti lions were struck down by an outbreak of canine distemper that probably started among the domestic dog population (there are said to be more than 100,000 such dogs running semi-wild around the Mara–Serengeti) and spread rapidly, facilitated by the lions' social way of life. Members of a pride lick and groom one another, and feed and fight together at kills, hastening the transmission of any disease. In all 1,000 lions died – one third of the population – though remarkably they have since bounced back, testimony to their ability to recover from such crises. Ironically, their demise initially led to an increase in the cheetah population on the Serengeti plains, but now, with lion numbers back to former levels, the cheetahs are starting to decline again.

A few years earlier, when rabies struck the Mara–Serengeti, it wreaked havoc among the wild dogs and was then compounded by an outbreak of canine distemper. This resulted in the loss between 1989 and 1992 of all eight radio-collared packs, many of which had been the focus of my book. Wild dogs are the most social of carnivores and go through a frenetic greeting ritual each morning and evening, with individuals licking into each other's mouths – a potent form of disease transmission that makes a pack equivalent to a single animal. Since that time, efforts have been made to inoculate the domestic dogs, but it is a massive undertaking.

The cheetah's wide-ranging habits and generally solitary lifestyle make it far less susceptible to epidemic diseases, helping to offset the mass die-offs seen in captive-breeding centres where these cats are kept in unnaturally high densities. In fact, the continued existence of the cheetah proves that it is a survivor, capable of re-building its population after a near-collapse. Most of the damage to a population that passes through a bottleneck occurs in the first few generations, so the cheetah's survival of that episode in its history can be thought of as a remarkable success story, particularly when one considers how many other species went extinct.

One suggestion that has been put forward as a way of increasing genetic variability among the cheetah population is to crossbreed or hybridize the East and southern African subspecies. In the early 1980s wildlife photographers Karl and Katherine Amman (Karl has since gone on to become a passionate spokesman for the plight of the world's great apes and for highlighting the threat that the bush-meat trade represents to Africa's wildlife) spent over a year investigating the possibility of introducing cheetahs from Namibia into Kenya – and in particular the Masai Mara – but the idea was eventually abandoned. There are a number of problems inherent in translocating predators into areas where they already exist, not least the fact that they may receive a hostile reception from residents: most cats are territorial and will fight or even kill non-residents. An intimate knowledge of an area gleaned from being brought up there gives residents a head start in life, and even though many subadults eventually leave their natal range they generally disperse gradually. A cat's first response to being translocated is usually to try to find its way home, often with disastrous consequences. Another problem is that all animals develop a degree of immunity to diseases typically found on their home turf, so translocating them may expose them to novel diseases to which they have no resistance.

But if the threat of epidemic diseases wasn't perhaps as serious as had first been thought, there were more surprises to come from O'Brien's detective work. When he and his associates examined semen from 18 of the 80 captive cheetahs at De Wilt, the concentration of sperm was only a tenth of that found in domestic cats, and the motility was slightly lower, very different from other species O'Brien had studied. More worrying still was that 70 per cent of the sperm showed abnormalities in shape (in domestic cats the figure is just under 30 per cent), with the flagella that propels the sperm often being coiled or bent at right angles. This might be expected greatly to reduce the chances of an egg being fertilized – in species such as domestic bulls, sperm abnormalities of as little as 10–20 per cent indicate that an animal is subfertile. Abnormalities of this kind are also often seen in highly inbred animals such as laboratory animals and domestic stock.

Wild dogs hunting on the Serengeti plains, bunching up to make it more difficult for the prey to distinguish their outline, and getting as close as possible before beginning to chase.

Adolescent cheetah chasing a young hyena that had been checking to see if the cheetahs had made a kill that it could steal.

At last it seemed that there was a plausible physiological reason why cheetahs suffered such high rates of juvenile mortality, and why they were so difficult to breed in captivity. O'Brien reported: 'The sperm data collected at De Wilt provided the first clue to the nature of the cheetah's plight.'

It was against this scientific backdrop that Karen Laurenson, a young English scientist who had completed a veterinary degree at Cambridge University, arrived in the Serengeti in the late 1980s to begin her PhD studies. Her aim was to learn more about life in the cheetah den. O'Brien's work on genetics had added another strand to the array of difficulties a cheetah mother faces when raising young in the wild. The time was ripe for someone to make a thorough investigation of this aspect of their biology, to discover how many cubs were being born to each female and the reasons for any deaths. Was there, for instance, any sign of cubs being born with a higher than expected incidence of birth defects?

The key to the study was to radio-collar a number of cheetahs, so that they could be relocated and followed on a regular basis, allowing pregnant females to be tracked to their dens. But radio-collaring wild animals – particularly in parks and reserves which attract large numbers of visitors eager to experience 'wild' Africa – has always been a contentious issue. Losses in the Mara–

Serengeti in the late 1980s and early 1990s prompted some researchers to wonder whether handling and radio-collaring the wild dogs might not have stressed them sufficiently to make them more vulnerable to disease. However, this issue has since been carefully investigated and the use of radio collars is vigorously defended by most of the scientific community. There is no doubt that great care needs to be taken whenever intervention is deemed necessary, particularly with endangered species such as wild dogs and cheetahs. But equally it would be impossible to keep track of such far-ranging species and obtain such detailed information without the use of collars which, contrary to popular opinion, do not appear to alter the study animals' behaviour nor to bother them unduly.

During her three years in the field Laurenson saw at first hand just how difficult it is for a cheetah to raise cubs to maturity. I sometimes accompanied her as she tracked a mother with cubs and was amazed that any of the young survived, particularly when their den was in the middle of the grasslands. Perhaps the cats know better, though, and it is safer here

This lioness killed a black-backed jackal pup, but then abandoned it. Lions kill other predators as competitors, not for food.

than in the more sheltered places where larger predators lie up. But regardless of where a cheetah chooses to have her cubs, the majority of deaths are attributed to lions and hyenas – and predators are only one facet of the obstacles that face them

As Joy Adamson had reported from her observations of Pippa, one way that a mother cheetah – or a female leopard or lion for that matter – tries to avoid losing her cubs to predators is to move them every few days, although all the lairs are usually within an area of about 1km² (⅖sq. mile). All predators are quick to recognize what is going on in their area, and it doesn't make sense for a cheetah mother to be too predictable in her movements. Lions and hyenas can read the signs of deception as well as any sleuth; untoward behaviour is likely to be noticed and prompt them to investigate. Hyenas have such a finally tuned sense of smell – and lions can read scent well enough, too – that they may pick up on a cheetah's scent and decide to track her down as they go about their business.

Consequently a cheetah mother moves with the utmost caution, often not even leaving the den for an hour or two first thing in the morning, so as to allow any hyenas and lions time to settle before she heads off to hunt, returning again in the middle of the afternoon or at dusk. She continually stops and scans the surrounding country for signs of danger before finally joining her cubs, lying so flat in the grass or under a bush that she simply vanishes from view. If she feels threatened, she may even slink away again before reaching her destination – keeping low to the ground, adopting the same posture she would use when trying to avoid a human on foot.

Lions are particularly belligerent adversaries, with a penchant for bullying and harassing all the other predators, and they account for up to 75 per cent of cheetah cub mortality at the den. The lions' aggressive behaviour is no doubt motivated by competition for food and space, and

they show no mercy to their smaller rivals, exhibiting all the hostility that they display when attacking lions from neighbouring prides. The tendency of male lions to commit infanticide when they take over a new pride so that they can breed with the females might predispose them to kill the young of their competitors, though lionesses can be just as ruthless when defending their territory. One thing is certain, a cheetah that makes itself openly visible to lions is courting disaster, and cheetahs understandably treat lions with the utmost respect.

Hyenas meanwhile seem to kill cheetah cubs as just one more source of food. If a hyena approaches a cheetah den when the mother is in the area she will defend it by bluff and threat, hissing and lunging towards the predator, even at times slapping and biting at her larger opponent's rump in her attempts to force it to flee or to chase her, thereby leading it away from the cubs in the hope that they can make good their escape. Sometimes this ploy works, but at other times it simply arouses suspicion, and if a lion or hyena is really intent on investigating or attacking nothing will stop it.

Even though Laurenson's findings were based on data from a small number of

females, they did prove just how dangerous lions and hyenas are for cheetah cubs, as well as highlighting the hazards posed by grass fires and rainstorms that can cause the loss of entire litters while a mother is away hunting. I once saw this for myself when a massive grass fire swept through high stands of long grass in the west of the Serengeti during the dry season, obliterating the sun with a thick pall of smoke and ash, turning the plains into a wasteland within hours. Frogs, insects, snakes and tortoises were burned alive, and so too was at least one litter of four cheetah cubs that Laurenson had been observing at their grass den. We watched as their mother searched the area, unable to comprehend what had happened.

Other cubs die because they are abandoned. Sometimes it becomes just too stressful for a mother to find sufficient prey close to where she has established her den, particularly in places like the Serengeti where the cheetah's main prey – the Thomson's gazelle – is migratory, sometimes forcing her to trek tens of kilometres to secure a meal. A lactating cheetah must hunt – and hunt successfully – virtually every day, almost doubling the amount she normally eats in order to sustain her milk production. Under these

Hyenas feeding on a wildebeest they had killed at dawn along Rhino Ridge. Hyenas in the Mara live in clans of 30–50 individuals, defending their territory against other clans.

Grass fires are one of the many hazards that cheetahs face. The mother of these cubs was visibly distressed when she returned to the area having been away hunting; she searched and called for her family, apparently unable to understand what had happened.

taxing circumstances she may have no alternative but to abandon her litter. This may seem harsh, but with a cheetah's ability to come into season every twelve days – or even less – and a gestation period of just three months, it may be better to try again and hope for more favourable conditions.

Another important finding to emerge from Laurenson's work was that congenital defects among wild cheetahs were very rare. Of 125 cubs studied, only two died of birth abnormalities, a reassuringly low number considering how inbred the population is. But the impact of predation proved to be greater than anyone had previously thought. Even when cubs are mobile enough to follow their mother, they are still highly vulnerable. Laurenson found

that 40 per cent of those that survived life at the den perished during the next month. It was becoming apparent that the Serengeti cheetahs were being suppressed by an increase in the populations of their greatest enemies – the lions and hyenas. Thanks to years of good rainfall and an increase in their food supply (there are currently 1.5 million wildebeest, 200,000 zebras and more than 400,000 gazelles in the

Four two-week-old cheetah cubs in a den in the Serengeti. In this case the 'den' was nothing more than a depression in the grass made by the mother's body.

Mara–Serengeti ecosystem, an area of 25,000km² (almost 10,000sq. miles), the population of these two predators is at an all-time high – nearly 3,000 lions and 9,000 hyenas. The fact that both cheetahs and wild dogs are such competent hunters, with a higher success rate than lions, hyenas or leopards, must be a factor in their ability to survive here – they can always hunt again if they lose their kill to a more powerful adversary.

If greater predation on cheetah cubs is the reason for the recent decline in the number of large litters seen in the Serengeti, we still do not know whether a decrease in fertility due to inbreeding is causing cheetahs to give birth to smaller litters than in the past – though if litter sizes in Nairobi Park are anything to go by, the answer would have to be no. The fact that cheetahs had proved so difficult to breed in captivity – fewer than 25 per cent of adults breed more than once – initially reinforced concerns about this very issue. But it seems that those worries were largely misplaced, proving just how important it is to study animals in their natural habitat, as well as in captivity and in the laboratory. Low testosterone levels in male cheetahs turned out to be a feature of both captive and wild populations. Captive cheetahs that had bred and those that had not showed no difference in testosterone levels or in sperm abnormalities, thereby ruling out these factors as possible reasons for poor captive breeding.

Today 10 per cent of the world's cheetah population – 1,376 individuals in 2001 – live in captivity, but only 5 per cent of these breed successfully. Although the number of births has increased over the past 50 years, these are still outstripped by deaths and the captive population is declining by 5 per cent a year. Currently, only 8 per cent of captive-breeding facilities worldwide have managed to breed cheetahs and have until now relied on the fact that 30 per cent of all captive cheetahs are wild caught. Low reproductive success and high infant mortality remain features of captive-breeding programmes – over 30 per cent of cubs do not survive their first six months. Here the problem has nothing to do with predators; instead deaths occur because of a multitude of causes such as infections, stillbirths, cannibalism, congenital defects, hypothermia and maternal neglect.

Long before O'Brien's work on cheetah genetics was published, George Schaller had voiced his doubts about the propriety of housing male and female cheetahs together in captivity, something that was then common practice in zoos. He pointed out that adult cheetahs avoided each other in the wild, that males and females met only occasionally and did not form a lasting pair bond, and that both sexes were promiscuous, with males associating with females only to mate or to test if they were in oestrus. It is now standard practice to house male and female cheetahs separately, bringing them together only when a female is in oestrus, even allowing her the chance to consort with more than one male in an effort to induce the best result. Though it is true that adult cheetahs mainly avoid contact with one another, a male cheetah was seen to feed from a kill that Kike had made while she was still accompanied by three large cubs; leopard females are also sometimes forced to share their kill with the territorial male.

While breeding cheetahs in captivity remains problematical, wild cheetahs breed perfectly well. Data from the Serengeti Cheetah Project's work shows that 95 per cent of the females studied reproduced. A female cheetah comes into oestrus on average every twelve days, though it can be up to three weeks. Normally she does not appear to come into oestrus while she is accompanied by small cubs (or does not choose to mate during this period), though one captive female was observed to come into season while her cubs were only four months old. A cheetah who loses her cubs quickly comes back into oestrus, and one female was seen accompanied by males the same day as she had lost a litter. It is possible for a female to conceive again as little as two days after losing her cubs, though the average is more like three weeks. The interval between litters whose cubs survive is somewhat shorter in cheetahs than in either lions or leopards, usually 15–18 months, and as with leopards a cheetah female will often mate again before her cubs are independent. It appears that cheetahs are supremely adapted to maximize their reproductive potential, no doubt because of the high losses they sustain in rearing cubs, with young females capable of becoming pregnant within six months of leaving their mother, coming into oestrus within days of losing cubs – or within weeks of their cubs becoming independent – and continuing to breed until they die. Even the oestrus cycle is compressed in time, lasting for just three days – sometimes only a day if mating takes place.

A mating pair usually stays together for only a day or two, rather than engaging in the extended four-to-five-day bouts of copulation seen in lions and leopards. Mating in lions has been well documented and is not an uncommon sight on safari, but cheetah mating has been witnessed only rarely in the wild and perhaps takes place more commonly at night. Having said that, a number of drivers in the Mara have seen cheetahs mating, and all of them reported how infrequently they copulated.

An adult male cheetah will approach any female he has tracked down or come across by chance, regardless of whether or not she is accompanied by cubs, presumably to check on her reproductive status. He often stalks towards her from a distance as if hunting prey, then may break into a run, rushing in, ears pinned back, mouth tense, in an intimidating display. The female initially does her best to keep the male (or males) at bay, uttering a characteristic series of high-pitched yelps of appeasement. Both sexes may growl, chirp and whine as the male stalks around the female trying to get close enough to investigate her scent. If a coalition of males finds an oestrus female they may compete for the chance to mate with her, though not with the same level of violence that sometimes ensues with male lions in a similar situation. When that happens blood may be spilled before one of the lions prevails and 'takes possession' of the female, guarding her closely while his companions are left to lick their wounds – and perhaps wait their turn.

The larger and older Blond Male mating with a Marsh lioness. When a female is in oestrus lions copulate hundreds of times over the course of four or five days.

When more than one male cheetah is present they often surround the female, sometimes even pinning her to the ground. In one instance reported by Mel and Fiona Sunquist, a coalition of male cheetahs competed for a female by pushing each other off her with their heads whenever one of them tried to mount. Sarah Durant, who currently heads the Serengeti Cheetah Research Project, has seen cheetahs mating just once. On that occasion a coalition of three males cornered a female and all four disappeared into a bush. After a few seconds Durant saw what she described to a *National Geographic* writer as 'stacked cheetahs', with all three males mounted one atop the other and the female 'looking rather squashed' on the bottom.

Even when there is only one male involved, a brief scrap usually ensues as he makes contact with the female; both animals leap high into the air and slap at each other as the female attempts to ward the male off. Similarly hostile displays have been witnessed when male and female leopards meet, and may play a part in bringing a female into oestrus – if she is not already; they may be a prerequisite to successful mating. They may equally be a reflection of the fact that males and females meet infrequently. At the very least the altercation often induces the female to pee or give off scent, while the male carefully investigates the area where she has been lying or sitting. He may then display the typical flehmen face that all cats show when testing any strange scent, raising his head with mouth open – though in less dramatic fashion than a lion or leopard – drawing droplets of vapour-laden odour into his mouth so that he can 'read' her sexual status by means of the organ of Jacobson, an area of nerve-rich sensory cells that open via two small pits in the roof of all cats' mouths just behind their front incisors.

Not surprisingly, any cubs that may be present appear confused by these aggressive encounters and are likely to chirp in appeasement. The male usually ignores them, but if they start milling about or try to approach him he may lash out, though not normally aggressively enough to inflict a serious injury. One might expect males to try to kill cubs in a situation like this – infanticide has been reported for a number of other species of cat. Angie and I once saw a three-year-old male leopard track down and kill Half-Tail's two three-week-old cubs in Leopard Gorge, biting each one in the neck and then carrying them off, perhaps to eat them. Lions, cougars, tigers, Canadian lynxes, ocelots and feral domestic cats all indulge in infanticide, and far from being some aberrant form of behaviour, it seems to be the norm. It is certainly advantageous to new males, being the most efficient way for newcomers to gain access to females in their area and prompt them to mate. Killing cubs also reduces competition when resources are scarce, helping to provide a favourable environment for any cubs the new male or males might sire. Otherwise

they might have to wait as long as a year and a half – the time it takes for lion and leopard cubs to become sufficiently independent to allow their mother to raise her next litter – for the chance to mate and to sire cubs of their own.

The one exception to this pattern seems to be the cheetah, though I once saw a mother cheetah lose a litter in rather suspicious circumstances. I cannot be certain that the male I had seen prowling around her den did in fact kill her cubs, but I do know that they were never seen again.

The most persuasive explanation of why male cheetahs don't kill cubs is that females range over such large areas. Any male who killed a litter in the mother's absence could not be sure that he would be able to find her again and breed with her. Similarly, if more than one male in a cheetah coalition mated with the same female, none of them could be sure who sired any cubs born – there is no point in killing cubs that might be your own offspring.

Because cheetahs in the wild did not seem to be suffering from any untoward effect of their low genetic variability, some ecologists questioned the validity of O'Brien's work. First of all they maintained that it lacked an experimental control – O'Brien's team had used skin grafts from domestic cats, which were duly rejected by the cheetahs and vice versa, because there was no outbred cheetah population to control with. Perhaps more profoundly, some people argued that ecological factors such as loss of habitat and predation were more significant to the cheetah's survival than genetic diversity, and that there was no apparent evidence that the cheetah's decline – or that of any other species – was a result of genetic shortcomings.

However, O'Brien's work has recently been corroborated by a study undertaken at the University of California Santa Cruz (UCSC) on a small, squat, colonial-living rodent known as the pocket gopher that scurries around in burrows in the American

West. Researchers found that individuals from populations of pocket gophers showing little genetic variation accepted skin grafts from one another in the same way as cheetahs. These findings were backed up by the fact that gophers from a population with greater genetic variation rejected skin grafts from their neighbours. While not addressing the other concerns raised by O'Brien's critics, this does show that inbred mammals may be so genetically similar that their immune system is unable to distinguish between self and non-self – hence their acceptance of skin grafts from one another. Until now, nobody had found another wild animal that could accept skin transplants so readily from a member of its own species. As M. A. Sanjayan, one of the researchers at UCSC, noted,

Genetic variation is the stuff of evolution; it allows a population to adapt effectively to changes in the environment. You exist at a price if you have low genetic variation. It's like having lots of clones of yourself…. That doesn't bode well for disease resistance. If a new disease arises, either they'll all be resistant or they'll all be wiped out. You may not get a middle response, where at least some individuals make it. That is something you'd expect with other species.

Researchers are now investigating the effect of such low genetic variation among pocket gophers on disease resistance, physiological fitness and their survival in the wild, something that Laurie Marker and her associates at the Cheetah Conservation Fund are working on with cheetahs in Namibia. But more about that project later in the book. First let's take a closer look at work carried out on the cheetah in the Mara, a place where man's impact on predators is very evident.

*D*r Luke Hunter, who co-ordinated the successful reintroduction of cheetahs into Phinda Game Reserve in South Africa, a fenced sanctuary of 170km² (65sq. miles) – similar in size to Lake Nakuru and Nairobi National Parks in Kenya – was able to test the hypothesis that lions do not commit infanticide. *Phinda is an area of mixed bushveld dominated by acacia woodland. Between 1992 and 1994, 13 lions and 15 cheetahs were released into the area, joining leopards, hyenas, jackals, caracals, servals and a range of other predators. Two crucial factors helped to make the reintroduction a success: there were no resident lions or cheetahs for the newcomers to compete with, and the cats were given ample time to adjust to their new home before being released – a technique referred to as 'soft release'. Hunter and his colleagues were able to relocate the cheetahs through the use of radio collars, and found that males always approached females, regardless of whether or not they were accompanied by cubs. A male stayed with a female for anything from 20 minutes to 18 days. If she tried to escape he would attempt to stop her, sometimes pinning her down, with a great deal of vocalizing from both sexes. Females tended to growl and hiss, and if the males attempted to move closer would yip and churr. The males constantly yipped and stuttered, occasionally growling in response to the female's attempts to keep them at bay. Some observers say that both males and females stutter-bark and yip to locate a mate when a female is in oestrus.*

In my experience, if the female tries to leave a male's company, as she invariably does if she is not interested in mating – even when he appears to have lost interest in her or has satisfied himself as to her sexual receptiveness or lack of it – he may well come rushing back, and the whole process of intimidation and sniffing for scent starts all over again. Eventually, sometimes hours later, the female is able to lead her cubs away and the male continues on his chosen path – unless she is in season.

What was very apparent from Hunter's observations, apart from the surprising level of aggression shown by males towards females (prompted it seems in part by the females' lack of interest in mating), was how unconcerned the males seemed to be with any cubs present. They certainly did not perceive them as a threat, nor make any attempt to kill them, and seemed primarily preoccupied with getting close to the mother, almost as if they were trying to kidnap her. For their part, the cubs alternated between the desire to flee, to keep close to their mother and even to approach the male. Hunter found no evidence of males trying to kill cubs. He also feels that the high levels of cub mortality seen on the Serengeti plains, where cubs are very visible when they start to follow their mother, are the most extreme losses experienced by a cheetah population. In the closed woodlands of Phinda, 70 per cent of cubs survive to independence.

Nick harassing Amber's daughter – typical behaviour when a male cheetah is trying to establish whether or not a female is in oestrus. These fights rarely cause injuries, bar the odd scratch or bite, though in this instance Nick ended up with a bloody nose.

The Mara

Not long after I came to live in the Mara in 1977, a young American couple, David and Lida Burney, began a year-and-a-half study of the cheetah population in and around the reserve. David was working towards his Masters degree, focusing on the ecological, behavioural and population biology of cheetahs, with particular emphasis on the impact of human activities on these cats. Research of this type requires at least two people full-time, and David and Lida worked very much as a team, with Lida as chief driver and compiler of the photographic record that enabled them to identify individual cheetahs.

Though none of us knew it at the time, the recent border closure imposed by Tanzania was going to transform the Mara from a little-known wildlife sanctuary to the jewel of Kenya's tourist industry. The Mara had always lived in the vast shadow of the Serengeti, a great swathe of country almost ten times its size, made famous the world over by the book and Oscar-winning film *Serengeti Shall Not Die* by the German naturalists Michael and Bernhard Grzimek. By the time visitors reached the Kenya border and the Mara after a safari through northern Tanzania, they could count on having seen black-maned lions in the Ngorongoro Crater, leopards lolling in yellow-barked fever trees along the Seronera River and perhaps even the thrill of a cheetah kill around Gol Kopjes. Now they were ready to head home, with just time for a quick stopover in the Mara to ease the journey back to Nairobi via the flamingo-pink paradise of Lake Nakuru a few hours short of the city.

I well remember the impact the border closure had on tourist facilities such as Mara River Camp, where I was based. Suddenly visitors who had been looking forward to enjoying the sight of massive herds of wildebeest spread across the Serengeti's famous short-grass plains found themselves on an extended stay in the Mara, a place they had probably never heard of before. Almost overnight the camp was running at full capacity and we were all concerned about whether the Mara would be able to offer a rich enough experience to counter the disappointment of guests who would no longer be visiting the Serengeti. But we need not have worried – the Mara is an exceptional game-viewing area too, and there is nothing like a piping hot shower taken under the stars to welcome you back to camp, before you sit down to a hearty dinner cooked over an open fire.

Despite a boom in its economy, Kenya faced problems. By the time I arrived in the country, poaching – as in many parts of Africa – was out of control; elephants and rhinos were being slaughtered on a massive scale and so too were leopards. The cheetah's spotted skin meant that it did not escape unscathed either. Though not as highly prized as a leopard pelt, during the height of the fur trade in the 1960s 1,500 cheetah skins were imported from Africa into the United States alone. Within a few months of the border closure, Kenya banned trophy hunting and the sale of all wildlife products, shutting down the lucrative curio-shop business that had until

The 1,500 elephants in and around the Mara can be a problem for farmers, destroying crops and endangering peoples' lives.

now made Nairobi a shopper's paradise, a marketplace full of semi-precious stones, wood carvings and ivory. From that time up to the present day, Kenya has resisted all calls to introduce the consumptive use of wildlife – game cropping and trophy hunting – preferring to promote tourism as a way of helping to pay the heavy price of conserving its predators and prey. This is in marked contrast to many southern African countries, where game farming and trophy hunting are a long-established way of making a living from wildlife – and in the best case scenarios of helping to protect wildlife on private land. With 70 per cent of Kenya's wildlife reportedly living on private land, the government is under increasing pressure to review its position on consumptive utilization.

By the mid-1980s, the Mara was hosting 200,000 visitors a year (the figure would eventually rise to 300,000 in the late 1980s before falling away again), with a massive proliferation of tented camps and lodges. Old hunting camps such as Mara Sara, just downstream from my base at Mara River, transformed themselves into luxury tented camps responding to the boom in photographic safaris. Further upstream, Mara Buffalo Camp, and later on Mara Safari Lodge, catered for visitors to the triangle of land between the Mara River, the main road leading to Nairobi, and Aitong Hill – prime cheetah habitat. In hindsight the Burneys' cheetah study was timely, coming as it did at a time of great change, and even today, almost 30 years later, it makes interesting and relevant reading.

David and Lida set up their camp under a beautiful fig tree near the Oloololo Gate, which provides access to the Mara Triangle – that part of the reserve located to the west of the Mara River and bounded to the west by the Siria Escarpment where Angie and I were married, which towers 300m (1,000ft) above the plains, and to the south by the border with Tanzania and the Serengeti. This area receives the highest rainfall of anywhere in the Mara and has always been exceptional cheetah country, but when the Burneys were conducting their study there were far fewer vehicles patrolling the Triangle than there are now, and consequently many of the cheetahs were shy and would slink away at the first sign of visitors on a morning game drive. A number of the cheetahs the Burneys glimpsed through their spotting scope were hurrying away up the stony face of the escarpment, venturing into the large tract of Masailand which extends north towards the village of Lolgorien, where I would sometimes go to fetch drinking water or other supplies for the camp. Occasionally I saw wild dogs in this area, trotting through the thickets alongside the muddy road, searching for impalas or gazelles. But I rarely saw cheetahs here.

I often met David and Lida, and like all the drivers and guides roaming the Mara's rolling plains and dappled acacia country, I was always keen to know the location of any cheetahs they had seen, adding their sightings to the rapidly burgeoning collection of field notes that I entered in my diary. To this day I still keep records of everything of interest that happens in Mara. My main priority then was to keep track of the movements and activities of the Marsh Lions on the other side of the river, and the elusive leopard was never far from my thoughts. But part of my role at Mara River Camp was to take visitors on game drives, and the best place to search for cheetahs in those early days was the area between the camp and Aitong Hill some 30km (20 miles) to the east. This was – and is – a beautiful stretch of country, sparsely populated by Masai pastoralists and their cattle. The dense stands of acacia woodland bordering camp thin as you crest the rise where we had carved out a rough bush airstrip. The plains roll and undulate like an giant ocean wave, enclosed on one side by the Mara River which rises 60km (36 miles) to the north in a shallow swamp among the dwindling stands of trees known as the Mau Forest.

The land here was divided into blocks by a series of luggas, intermittent watercourses that provided pools of water where the animals could slake their thirst. During the two annual rainy seasons the luggas were transformed into torrents of muddy-brown water, forcing you to add kilometres to your journey in an attempt to find a place where it was safe to cross. They used to be choked with patches of croton bush or sharp-thorned acacias, perfect resting places for lions and leopards, though in recent years the combined effect of elephants and fires – and the cutting of acacia bush by the Masai to make predator-proof cattle bomas – have opened up the countryside. As you moved within view of the Mara River, these high plains merged into rocky hillocks dotted with giant fig trees, African greenhearts and eleaodendrons. If you were lucky you might find a fresh kill hanging from a leopard's larder, though in those days leopards were so shy that a carcass was all you were likely to see. The closer you got to the blue mass of Aitong Hill the wider the animal-spotted plains became – a green table-top carpeted with topis, wildebeest, zebras, impalas and gazelles. This was as fine a stretch of cheetah country as you could hope to find, even rivalling the Triangle in those days.

The Burneys found that cheetahs appeared to be thriving both in and out of the reserve, though surprisingly perhaps the population density in their primary study area was twice as high outside the protected area. Cheetahs seemed to co-exist well with the way in which the Masai used these rangelands, and other subsistence activities in the area had little or no obvious effect on them. At the time, development in the region was being boosted by large World Bank loans, and the Burneys felt that wheat farming, organized ranching and capital improvements on the access roads from population centres might affect the cheetahs in the future, as has proved to be the case.

The Mara is bordered to the north, east and west by land so similar to that inside the reserve that most people would not realize that they had travelled beyond the boundary. In the 1970s there wasn't even the occasional concrete bollard standing out among the grasslands to mark the extent of the reserve, and certainly no-one mentioned that one day the Mara might have to be fenced off from the surrounding pastoral land. But recently one of our local newspapers carried an article lobbying for the fencing off of the Mara Triangle to

prevent animals from wandering onto private land and destroying crops or endangering lives. Elsewhere in Kenya putting up fences to keep the wildlife in and people out is a well-established practice. Nakuru National Park is already surrounded by an electric fence, and the Aberdares is entering the final phase of being fenced off.

Nairobi National Park has been in and out of the news as demands for it to be fenced on all sides have intensified (currently there is an open corridor to the east allowing the animals to move back and forth seasonally). At the heart of the controversy are the famous lions, whose preservation was one of the reasons for establishing the area as Kenya's first national park in 1946. In the last few years the lion population has plummeted from around 35 to just 9, due to Masai herdsmen killing them in retaliation for

Chui sheltering behind a croton bush. Unlike cheetahs, leopards do everything possible to avoid exposing themselves to view.

Five seven-month-old cheetahs in the Mara Triangle, where the distinctive balanites or 'desert dates' speckle the plains and provide a shady resting place during the hottest part of the day.

livestock losses and sometimes simply to draw attention to the issue of compensation for deaths due to predators. Many of the people living in the Kitengela dispersal area outside Nairobi Park would like to be able to collect firewood and grass for thatching – and to bring their cattle into the park during times of drought. The fear is that if the park isn't fenced it may eventually be lost to development.

A mother cheetah and cubs using an abandoned Masai house as a look-out, just as they would a termite mound or vehicle.

A Masai manyatta – home of the warriors – near Amboseli National Park in the shadow of Mount Kilimanjaro.

The pressure for such action will surely intensify as the human population grows and the demand for land increases around the Mara. The days when wild animals shared the northern rangelands with nomadic pastoralists in relative harmony are drawing to a close. The Masai are becoming more sedentary, with corrugated iron replacing the more traditional roofing of cow dung or thatch, and they now rely for their sustenance almost entirely on maize and other arable crops that they must either buy or cultivate for themselves. Agriculture in particular will spell the end of the game in Masailand.

During my first year in the Mara I quite often bumped into a family of cheetahs close to camp. Driving out each morning I would stop on a high point to scan the land ahead with my binoculars, switching off my vehicle's engine so that I could listen to the sounds of the wilderness, hoping that I might hear lions roaring and get a fix on their position, keeping my ears open for the alarm calls of jackals or vervet monkeys that usually meant a leopard had been spotted by these sharp-eyed prey animals, or straining my eyes to pick out a cheetah's distinctive silhouette.

This family of cheetahs – a mother and three nine-month-old cubs – was the same one that the Burneys focused on. It traversed a large home range of about 100km² (40sq. miles). Another female cheetah with three cubs overlapped part of the same area and though both were habituated to vehicles, it was the first family that I spent most of my time watching. The two females were distinctive enough in their appearance and behaviour for me to tell them apart, and their cubs were of different ages. I knew the first mother simply as the Mara River Camp female, and her cubs became so used to vehicles that they eventually took to climbing up onto the roof, though their mother never did.

In those days it was not unusual to see a cheetah with three or even four large cubs, so the rate of survival was reasonably good, and it was evident that the cheetahs living beyond the reserve boundary raised more young. There were a number of reasons for this, not least the fact that they shared the area with the Masai pastoralists. With human population densities being low and the Masai still adopting a semi-nomadic way of life, the wild herbivores flourished according to the seasons, prospering in wet years and retreating again during periods of drought. For the cheetahs prey was plentiful and competition from other large predators at a minimum because of the presence of the Masai. It was rare for cheetahs to lose their kills to hyenas or lions, though I did once see one of the Marsh Pride males steal a warthog kill from the mother cheetah, having been alerted from his resting place among a patch of forest by the squeals of the piglet. But this was the exception.

Despite the fact that cheetahs are mainly active during the daytime, they rarely attempt to take livestock in this part of Masailand, though an unprotected sheep or goat would be considered fair game. They prefer to hunt for themselves and rarely scavenge from a kill made by another predator. Unlike the crafty and opportunistic leopard, cheetahs do not come skulking round a cattle boma in the dead of night or pose the threat that lions and hyenas do to people and livestock. In this they are indeed fortunate. The Masai's response to problem predators has always been ruthlessly efficient. In the case of wayward lions, a group of warriors and older men from one or more villages would gather to hunt down the offending predators, harrying them until the panic-stricken cats broke from cover, giving the warriors the opportunity to spear them. When livestock has been killed almost any lion will do and a fine-maned Mara male would be a bonus, the traditional symbol of bravery, his death bringing honour to the age-set that killed him. Killing lions for ceremonial purposes – something that every generation of warriors aspired to in the olden days (and even today for that matter) – is now illegal. But killing a predator that threatens your life or livelihood is another matter, and is generally accepted around the world as being justified.

Hyenas are dealt with differently. They are coursers, not stalkers, and can easily outrun a man on foot – their loping stride

Hyenas squabbling at a kill. Hyenas are highly adaptable, capable of killing singly or in groups, of scavenging from kills made by other predators, and of hunting by day or at night.

is so efficient that they can gallop across the open plains for kilometre after kilometre without pausing for breath, refusing to bay up and stand their ground as a lion or leopard might do. The answer is simple enough: lace a carcass with cattle dip, a toxic solution that is cheap and easy to acquire and administer, then wait for the killers to return. The problem is that poison is indiscriminate – anything that eats from the carcass will be killed, whether it is a hyena, a lion, a leopard or a vulture.

Cheetahs are spared this kind of death because of their aversion to scavenging. They also have the speed to outrun any man. But men with dogs are a different matter. A pack of dogs can put the fear of God into the largest cat, and is capable of hounding even the fastest until it is winded.

When that happens the cat must either find a tree to scramble up or collapse exhausted and meet its fate. Now it is at the mercy of its human adversaries, be they armed with firearm, spear or bow and arrow. A year or so ago there was a report of herdsmen killing an adult cheetah, and boys with dogs sometimes chase and kill cheetah cubs. Such incidents were unheard of when the Burneys were studying cheetahs. In fact, far from being a threat to their survival, the presence of the Masai outside the boundary of the reserve indirectly helped the cheetahs to flourish by controlling lion and hyena numbers. These larger and potentially more dangerous predators were forced to lie low during daytime when the Masai were out and about, searching for good grazing for their herds.

The Masai are tolerant of wildlife as long as it does not interfere unduly with their pastoral lifestyle. They do not kill wild animals for food – cattle have always provided them with most of their needs: milk, blood and occasionally meat as food, cow hides for bedding, and dung to plaster the walls and roofs of their houses. This has allowed the cheetah's natural prey, the gazelles and impalas, to thrive alongside the Masai's livestock. As the most timid and least aggressive of the big cats, cheetahs are no threat to man and have never been known to attack humans in the wild – it is just not in their nature. They are not man-eaters and simply do not have the strength – or the inclination – to overcome an adult human. This is not to say that they are not capable of biting, scratching and inflicting a nasty wound – just look what a bundle of trouble a domestic cat can be when frightened and desperate to escape – and you could certainly lose a finger to a cheetah's razor-sharp carnassials.

Two of the Aitong males investigating a scent post and leaving their own pungent odour to help mark their territory.

My occasional meetings with cheetahs and their cubs quickly made me realize that they led a very different kind of life to the other two big cats, not least in the extent to which they wandered. I often found them 20–30km (12–18 miles) from where I had last seen them, and the four females that the Burneys located most commonly in the northern Mara occupied home ranges of anything from 40–140km² (15–55sq. miles), with an average of 80 km² (30sq. miles). This was larger than the territories of the lions and leopards I was following in this part of the Mara. In fact it was almost double the size of the Marsh Pride's territory and three times the area occupied by Chui, the leopard I wrote about in *The Leopard's Tale* and *Big Cat Diary: Leopard*. The Burneys found that one female with newborn cubs was much more localized in her movements and spent the first two weeks within a 2km² (¾sq. mile) area, adopting the same kind of restricted existence that I had seen leopards and lions follow when their cubs were tiny and at their most vulnerable. Male cheetahs had much smaller territories, with two males occupying ranges of 16 and 17km² (6¼ and 6½sq. miles), though the small sample size almost certainly produced an underestimate. Ronald McLaughlin found that the two resident cheetah families he studied in Nairobi National Park had home ranges of about 80km² (30sq. miles). These

The Marsh Pride resting in the shade of a gardenia bush near Bila Shaka Lugga. The Mara's burgeoning elephant population has drastically reduced the amount of cover for lions.

Honey and her cubs at Kichwa Tembo airstrip. She seemed totally unconcerned about the man on the tractor.

Once cubs start to follow their mother they barely let her out of their sight except when she is hunting. They reunite by responding to her calls and by calling themselves.

overlapped considerably, though the areas each frequented most often were more exclusive. The coalition of two males living in the park moved through the whole area.

What was very evident was that adult cheetahs and groups of newly independent young avoided close encounters with strangers, keeping a careful watch on any other cheetahs who came into view. With its sharp amber eyes, a cheetah is capable of spotting another cheetah from 5km (3 miles) away, giving them the opportunity to slip away and avoid conflict. It is rare to see a female cheetah scent-mark in typical cat fashion, arching her tail and spraying against a prominent scent-post, in the way that a female leopard does as she wanders around her territory. And that is the difference: cheetah females do not defend their home range – it is simply too large. But male cheetahs often mark the trunks of trees scattered throughout their range, and in so doing show all the appearances of staking out a territory. A male walking across an open grassy plain will often deviate to investigate a lone tree or fallen log, sniffing carefully to read any scent messages left by other male cheetahs who

have passed through the area, then abruptly wheeling round and dousing the spot with his own distinctive odour, created by spurts of urine mixed with pungent secretions from his anal glands.

However, although they do not defend a territory, females do leave scent as they move around, and both sexes often defecate on prominent places, most commonly fallen tree trunks or one of the many termite mounds that speckle the Mara's plains. A female's faeces contain traces of hormones that advertise her sexual state, and females apparently spray-mark and call with a strident 'yip' when they are in season. Recent improvements in endocrine tests of urine or stool samples can detect hormones indicating stress, oestrus, the breeding cycle or the time of an expected birth. The benefit of these new tests is that wild animals can be studied without being anaesthetized. They also hint at the complex array of messages that urine and faeces may convey from one cheetah to another.

The spacing system employed by cheetahs is similar in many ways to that used by their closest big cat relative, the

New World puma. Male pumas stake out territories with little or no overlap by scent-marking and visual avoidance, while females share areas with males and other females. This helps to reduce competition between males for females in season, and in this respect also resembles the system used by leopards.

By the end of their study, the Burneys estimated that 61 cheetahs aged over three months lived in the area customarily used by tourists visiting the Mara – including all of the reserve – with up to 70 in the best-case scenario. This figure was based on three study sites totalling 2,495km² (975sq. miles), 57 per cent of which was in the reserve, giving a density of one cheetah per 41km² (16sq. miles). They felt that there might be as many as a hundred cheetahs in the Mara region as a whole, with over twice as many living outside the reserve as within it. It was evident that the Masailand of south-western Kenya supported a viable cheetah population, with the Loita Plains to the east of the reserve providing a refuge for many cheetahs that were seldom if ever seen by tourists. At that time estimates from the Serengeti gave a density of about one per 80–100km² (30–40sq. miles) for the ecosystem, compared with one per 72km² (28sq. miles) in Kruger National Park in South Africa. So the Mara and particularly the surrounding rangelands were highly prized cheetah habitat. In Nairobi National Park, the density is even higher, at one cheetah per 10km² (4sq.

miles), demonstrating that where larger predators do not limit their numbers cheetahs reproduce well.

Apart from trying to discover whether the cheetah was rare because of any limit imposed by the habitat (it turns out that the cheetah can tolerate a broad range of habitats, as witnessed by its former wide distribution), the Burneys had been particularly keen to evaluate human impact on the population. They quickly discovered that harassment of animals was a real problem in the Mara – particularly for the big cats that everyone wanted to see and most particularly, it seemed, for the cheetahs.

Part of the reason was that there were very few permanent or well-maintained roads or tracks, and those that were distinct enough to stand out disappeared under a blanket of red-oat grass during the long rains. This meant that each vehicle was tempted to create its own pathway across the plains, guided by whatever animals they could find to satisfy the appetites of their visitors for close-up photography. Off-road driving such as this is still a feature of any safari to the northern Mara, despite the fact that it is now contrary to the reserve regulations (limited off-road driving is

Kike and cubs sitting out a rainstorm. After rain, cheetahs fastidiously groom their own coats and lick the rain from the coats of family members – an easy way of gaining moisture.

Once a storm has begun to blow over, cheetahs often take advantage of the conditions to stalk up on prey, particularly if it is facing away from them, hunched against the wind and rain.

permitted in the Mara Triangle, as discussed later) – it has been practised for so long that it is hard to break the habit and dissuade people from doing it. There just aren't sufficient anti-harassment patrols or vehicles to deal with the issue, and many people feel that driving off road is part of what makes a safari to the Mara unique. In a sense they are right. When we are filming *Big Cat Diary* we are given a special dispensation to drive off road – this is the norm for camera crews in most wildlife areas in Africa, and you pay a filming fee over and above your park entrance fee for the privilege. But there is a strong argument for greater restrictions in the Mara, where as many as 30 vehicles may aggregate at a cheetah or (more likely) a leopard sighting – and one researcher in Amboseli National Park found that more than six vehicles clustered around a cheetah sharply diminished their hunting ability.

The Burneys noted that tourist vehicles often pursued cheetahs in the Mara almost relentlessly throughout the day. And beyond the reserve boundary they have to

contend with man in his more traditional guise – on foot. One thing the Burneys quickly realized was that individual cheetahs vary markedly in their response to tourist vehicles. They cited the example of one male who frequented the Mara Triangle and whom they jokingly referred to as the Phantom. He was so shy that he would focus his attention on their vehicle from 300m (1,000ft) away and flee for cover if they attempted to move closer or the minute a second vehicle appeared. They used a x20 telescope to observe their study animals, usually from an elevated position in short grass so as not to affect their behaviour, and in order to keep far enough away not to attract other vehicles. The Phantom's favourite ploy was to run off up the Siria Escarpment where no vehicle could follow, or bury himself in high grass or a patch of bush, behaving more like a leopard than a cheetah, with his spotted coat mirroring the dappled light. Sometimes he continued up and over the rise where the Masai only infrequently grazed their sheep and goats, proving that

cheetahs are capable of keeping a low profile where necessary to avoid conflict with humans.

The only time the Burneys saw vehicles get close to the Phantom was when a group of minibuses chased and outflanked him on very open ground, approaching to within 50m (160ft) of the fleeing cheetah for a few seconds before he darted into thick bush and once again became invisible. They were fortunate that cheetahs are such timid creatures. While I was working on *The Leopard's Tale*, a group of tourist vehicles harassed a shy male leopard, forcing him to flee from cover into the open. He then turned on his assailants and charged, mauling one of the passengers who had the temerity to lean out of the open side of the vehicle to take his picture.

The story of the Phantom reminded me of a visit I made to the Serengeti shortly after the border had reopened in 1983. I stayed at Ndutu Lodge, where wildlife cameraman Hugo van Lawick camped for many years. Over a drink one evening we were discussing how wary many of the

Thunderstorms accompanied by heavy rain are not uncommon even during the 'dry' season in the Mara, one reason why the area provides such rich pastures for the animals.

predators were in certain parts of the Serengeti, partly as a result of the border closure, when tourism had all but dried up. In those days lions would sometimes trot away as vehicles approached, and so would cheetahs. One tour driver remarked to me that if a cheetah was shy and wandering in the open, it would soon tire if you chased it and be forced to lie down, allowing visitors the chance to take photographs.

Much as the Phantom was capable of keeping humans at bay, there were other cheetahs that seemed almost oblivious to humans in vehicles. One such was the Airport male, who chased and caught a Thomson's gazelle buck that had been grazing at the edge of Governor's Camp airstrip, bowling the prey over when it turned its head to look towards an aeroplane that was landing. In the course of

the afternoon five more planes landed and three took off, during which time the cheetah dragged his kill to within 25m (80ft) of the edge of the tarmac to utilize the meagre shade provided by a strip-marker. Six hours later all that remained were a few large bones and one very contented cheetah. Not surprisingly, the manner in which vehicles approached cheetahs had a marked effect on their reactions, and minibuses driven directly towards them at high speed prompted them to flee.

Many conservationists have expressed concern about the effect of tourist vehicles on the cheetah's wellbeing, even inside large protected areas. The Burneys' data indicated that heavy tourist pressure did lower hunting success, but that if there were plenty of small-to-medium-sized

antelopes within half a kilometre (⅓ mile) or so, even a harassed cheetah generally managed to kill, often during the middle of the day or when no tourists were visiting. Tamer individuals killed even when cars were present, especially if the cars remained stationary during the last tense moments of the hunt. Prey was often alerted by vehicle movement, forcing the cheetah to try again to narrow the distance separating it from its intended victim (though ironically the Burneys also found that the presence of vehicles sometimes distracted prey or provided cover, giving tamer cheetahs an advantage).

The Burneys had both worked in large parks in the United States and realized how difficult management decisions can be, especially when two species are involved and one of them is man. They often had to remind themselves that the tourist and the carnivore are dependent on one another, that the former finances the preservation of the latter. That is as true today as it was 30 years ago – the tourist's daily entrance fee helps to pay for the upkeep of East Africa's parks and reserves. Generations of cheetahs have now been raised in the presence of tour vehicles and the great majority are habituated enough to be viewed at close quarters. All that is needed is for people to treat them with respect and, once a cheetah is on the hunt, to watch from a distance rather than trying to follow it.

Cheetahs generally avoid the vicinity of camps and lodges, which attract baboons and hyenas keen to pilfer from the garbage dumps that such facilities spawn. They also tend to avoid people working on road and airstrip construction and general lodge maintenance, moving away or fleeing from anyone on foot at five to ten times the distance at which they would tolerate a vehicle. Ironically, the same construction sites and murram pits when shorn of their human inhabitants provide cheetahs with a convenient perch from which to view their surroundings, and large noisy construction vehicles often race past a cheetah as close as 25m (80ft) without provoking flight, despite the banging and crashing they make as they continue on their way.

Big Cat Diary donated a vehicle to the Mara Conservancy, a private management company that manages the Mara Triangle, to help with visitor surveillance, particularly where cheetahs are concerned, and Angie and I conducted a fund-raising event for Friends of Conservation during the launch of *Big Cat Diary: Leopard* to help purchase a second vehicle. Poaching does not seem to have affected cheetahs in the Mara to any great extent, even when the trade in spotted cat skins was at its peak in the 1960s and 1970s. Cheetahs are generally too quick and alert to be hunted down easily, unless by someone in a vehicle with a gun, and poaching from a vehicle in open country would be liable to detection in an

area as heavily visited as the Mara. And the fact that cheetahs avoid kills made by other predators makes them almost impossible to poison. One of the benefits of having a large number of tourists visit the Mara each year is that it helps to deter poachers – significantly, the Mara Triangle, which receives fewer visitors than other parts of the reserve, has traditionally had higher levels of poaching. As we shall see in Chapter 8, since the Mara Conservancy took over the day-to-day running of the Triangle there has been a significant reduction in poaching, which has to be a blessing for all the animals.

Since the time of the Burneys' study, people have become increasingly concerned by an apparent decline in cheetah numbers, particularly outside the reserve, with low sightings, stories of abandoned cubs and sick or injured individuals. In response to this, the Kenya Wildlife Service (under whose remit the wellbeing of all Kenya's animals falls), with funding from a number of sources, including Laurie Marker's Cheetah Conservation Fund, initiated in 2001 a census of cheetah numbers in and around the reserve. The findings make disturbing reading and indicate a reduction in the cheetah population from 61 in 1980 to a maximum of 45 today. During the year of the study, it was necessary to treat eight cheetahs, of which five had mange (a disease that can be spread through contact with domestic animals and is often a sign of stress), one had been wounded by a hyena while defending its kill, one had suffered a dislocation while hunting and one was old and needed medical attention. Eleven cheetahs were known to have

died – six of them killed by predators, three in conflict with pastoralists, one hit by a car and one of unknown causes.

With the increase in the number of people now living a more sedentary life close to the reserve boundary, the effect of far larger numbers of visitors, a reduction in poaching (which has benefited lions and hyenas more than cheetahs) and the worrying incidence of mange, there is little reason to doubt these findings.

Some of the cheetahs in the Mara have been given numbered ear-tags to help track their movements, a controversial decision in an area with so many tourists.

A cheetah called Amber

For a naturalist there is nothing more rewarding than gradually building up a relationship based on trust with a big cat, allowing you to see beyond its outward appearance. If you want to get intimate glimpses into the life of any creature – and photograph it – then you must learn to think as it does, absorbing every nuance of its behaviour. It took me six years to write my first book on leopards – that was how difficult it was to find a leopard I could watch, let alone photograph, in the 1970s. I had to ensure that whatever animal I was working with learned that my vehicle was no threat to her or her cubs, initially stopping a long way away and watching through binoculars, looking for signs that I could edge a little closer, using the longest telephoto lens I could afford to try to build up a record of their life. Since then I have been fortunate enough to be able to spend time with leopards such as Half-Tail and Zawadi – each different in character, each with her own idiosyncrasies and ways of being. It was while following Half-Tail that I became aware of a female cheetah who was causing great excitement among the drivers. They called her Queen, but Simon King re-christened her because of her large amber eyes and she became Amber to *Big Cat Diary* viewers.

Amber was as charismatic a character as Half-Tail – a cat with a difference. She behaved as if vehicles simply did not exist or were such a familiar part of her world that she no longer took any notice of them. You could see why the drivers had called her Queen – she had an air of such regal aloofness. I was entranced. Both Amber and Half-Tail were what the drivers called 'polite', 'well-mannered' cats, and they were tenacious in their loyalty to them. Woe betide anyone who treated them roughly or did not give them respect – not just other vehicles, but predators who might threaten them or their cubs. Amber and Half-Tail were like having money in the bank, helping to ensure that visitors went away happy. They were not to be taken lightly.

Amber's habit of leaping onto the bonnet of stationary vehicles simply added to her appeal, drawing gasps of surprise and delight, and sometimes shock or panic, from the occupants – this was after all a 'big cat'. But there was nothing threatening about her behaviour. She would stare into the distance, her large amber eyes scanning the horizon for potential prey or danger, particularly when she had cubs. Getting a better view of the surrounding area is all about survival, particularly in long grass, so when a cheetah becomes sufficiently confident to leap up onto a vehicle it gains an additional vantage point – one that is often higher than the termite mounds on which they are frequently seen – but with the added benefit in places like the Mara that vehicles tend to follow them around and so are often conveniently placed.

Amber was not unique in her car-climbing antics. Like lions, cheetahs in the Mara are exposed to vehicles from an early age and soon begin to explore these strange, noisy contraptions. With cubs this is nothing more than youthful exuberance;

Like Half-Tail, Amber was something of a legend in the Mara due to her complete acceptance of vehicles. She was easy to recognize because of a distinctive notch in her right ear.

they love to play on fallen logs or leap at the trunk of a tree, trying to scramble up it with varying degrees of success, and a tourist truck must seem like just another feature of their home range to be investigated and played with.

I have often wondered about the way in which cats distinguish between vehicles with people inside them and a person on foot. A vehicle masks the distinctive human outline or silhouette – and the distinctive human smell that many animals respond to with fear, either running away or charging and attacking. All young animals tend to be frightened by sudden movement or of an object heading towards them, and a man on foot spells possible danger – man the predator. Most animals wisely maintain a suitable flight distance between themselves and any predator on the move, keeping track of it and quickly moving off if the threat tries to approach. A shy leopard will leave the tree in which it has been resting

Kike exploring my Toyota Landcruiser. She treats vehicles just like termite mounds, and 'marks' them with her pungent droppings and urine.

and slink quietly away long before a vehicle can get close enough for people to take photographs, and it would certainly do the same if it saw a person walking towards it – without that person even knowing it was there. Lions will look up from their daytime slumber at the sound of Masai herdsmen approaching with their cattle, alerted by the high-pitched whistling of the herdboys and the cattle bells tinkling on the wind. This warning system works well for both man and animal, allowing predators to move off and avoid possible conflict.

The sound of human voices must have been a cause for alarm for wild animals

from the moment our ancestors started to walk upright and to hunt game. And presumably a man striding across the open savanna has been visible long enough for a genetic memory to be established, enabling an animal instinctively to take the appropriate avoidance action. Apart from any innate response they may have, young animals learn from their mother, and, in the case of lions and other social species, from association with other experienced individuals within their group. If a mother has become habituated to vehicles – or to people, for that matter – her young are likely to overcome their fear of these unfamiliar objects more quickly. Of course not all animals respond in the same way; some creatures – notably leopards – are generally shy by nature, because caution and secrecy are part of their hunting technique and help them to avoid larger predators.

Each animal is an individual, something that became very apparent to Angie and me while spending years working with leopards. Half-Tail was exceptionally tolerant of vehicles. In fact, over the years she seemed to become more accepting of people on foot as well, partly because she grew accustomed to seeing them get out of their cars and did not feel unduly

A mother cheetah and three cubs, aged five or six months, investigating the upper reaches of a balanites tree in the Mara Triangle.

Two of Kike's nine-month-old cubs peering over the roof of Angie's vehicle, intrigued by their mother's scent. Cubs progress from the spare wheel to clambering onto the roof.

threatened. Living as she did outside the Mara Reserve, she was also constantly exposed to the sight of Masai on foot. The drawback to this, of course, was that she became more vulnerable to anyone who might want to harm her. This was graphically illustrated when she was shot through the nose by a herdsman; there can't be many leopards who would let you get close enough to shoot them with a bow and arrow.

Half-Tail's daughter Zawadi was almost as carefree as her mother, yet for some reason Safi, the only cub that Zawadi reared to maturity, was always of a rather nervous disposition, far less bold than her brother, who was killed by lions when he was six months old. To this day Safi is still wary of vehicles and difficult to find.

The fact that cheetahs move and hunt during the daytime helps to facilitate this process of habituation. By the time they are three months old, the cubs are confident enough to scamper around vehicles, playing hide and seek and 'tag' under the cars, with their mother pacing around, keeping a watchful eye on them, joining in their games – or simply ignoring them. They chew and tear at anything within reach – strips of rubber tubing used to secure a high-lift jack, a kikoi (a traditional wrap-around garment) or hat left casually hanging from a door that gets caught in the wind and acts as a perfect plaything.

There is nothing exceptional about this, it is just cats being cats – a domestic kitten is similarly capable of turning anything into a toy or surrogate prey. But cheetahs grow particularly rapidly, enabling them to keep up with their mother from an early age, and their athletic leaps and bounds soon have them scrambling up onto the two spare tyres mounted on brackets on the back of many safari vehicles. The bonnet favoured by Amber as an adult is too much of an obstacle for the cubs' first climbing forays – tyres they can see and, having already clawed and bitten into the chewy black tread, they know what kind of surface they are leaping onto. From this perch it is only a matter of time before the cubs are large enough – at eight or nine months old – to peer inquisitively over the long expanse of a car roof. A month or two later they haul themselves up to the top for the first time, 2m (6ft 6in) or so above the ground.

Getting down is not so easy. When we filmed Kike during *Big Cat Week*, she sometimes descended by means of a single mighty leap. The cubs, on the other hand, may be forced to take their first tentative steps down onto the bonnet's shiny surface, skidding around like ducklings on a frozen pond.

When Amber's cubs became independent in late 1998, the two males

Knowing how delighted visitors would be to have Amber jump onto their car, drivers often drove into a good position to entice her onto the bonnet. She needed little persuading. In this respect 1998 proved a bonanza year for Simon and the cheetah crew. BCD audiences were thrilled to be able to watch a family of cheetahs clambering all over the filming vehicles, though we had to edit out an occasion when one of the cubs became overly inquisitive and reached forward to lick Simon on the head. Our reason for cutting this sequence was that we did not want people to misunderstand our relationship with the cheetahs. These are not pets, they are wild creatures, and the golden rule is not to touch them, however tempting it might be to stroke that spotted tail dangling in front of your nose through the roof hatch. It is imperative to preserve the natural divide between us and the big cats. If they start to feel that it is safe to make more intimate contact with human beings, they might run into trouble when they wander outside the reserve and encounter herdsmen who are naturally wary of predators and who might harm them if they allowed people to approach too close. Herdsmen may not always distinguish between one spotted cat and another, and the Masai consider the leopard both a nuisance and a danger.

Amber's two male cubs, aged 16 months, perched on one of the *Big Cat Diary* game-spotter vehicles.

stayed with their sister for another few months and it was noticeable that she was often the one who initiated a stalk and seemed to be more adept at hunting. It was also apparent that adolescent cheetahs of both sexes still have a lot to learn – they sometimes attempt to hunt right under the noses of hyenas. In addition to this, their success rate is not as good as that of adults, and it will be another year or so before they have mastered all the nuances that make adult cheetahs such masterful hunters.

Youngsters often target soft options such as newborn gazelles, young impalas, warthog piglets and hares. Staying together gives them more eyes and ears to detect danger, and hyenas are less likely to harass large groups of subadults. Angie and I saw Amber's sons wandering across Paradise Plain shortly after they had split up from their sister, traversing an area they had explored with their mother when they were cubs. They made no attempt to jump onto our vehicle and seemed far more concerned

with keeping a low profile. Perhaps they were wary about conflict with adult male cheetahs, who will sometimes attack and kill other males in defence of their territory. They ignored the solitary trees that adult males mark if they have claimed a territory. Young males such as these eventually leave their natal range, wandering up to 20km (12 miles) away before finding somewhere to settle. If they are lucky they may acquire a territory and, as many of the males in the Mara are singletons, these two had a good chance of being successful – though probably not until they were about four years old.

Amber's daughter stayed on in the area where she was born, sharing part of her mother's home range, typical behaviour for subadult female cheetahs and similar to the pattern of dispersal seen in leopards, where adult daughters often overlap part of their mother's range while avoiding using the same area at the same time.

Amber had an unusual history which helps to explain her familiarity with vehicles

and which dates back to the time of her mother's birth in July 1987. Her mother was one of a litter of five cubs born in a well-concealed outcrop of rock along a lugga bordering Rhino Ridge. Word soon spread of the cheetah family's whereabouts and they attracted a large following among the drivers of all the tented camps in the area. At the time I was based at Kichwa Tembo Camp in the Mara Triangle, a good hour's drive away over rough terrain, but the chance to see cheetah cubs was sufficient incentive for me to undertake the journey whenever I could.

The cubs spent much of their early life on the game-rich plains surrounding the Olare Orok and Ntiakitiak Luggas, an area much loved by private safari operators, who pitch their camps among the giant fig trees that line these beautiful tributaries of the Talek River. As the cubs grew they often climbed onto vehicles and were even petted and touched by over-enthusiastic visitors and drivers, something that would be discouraged today. But in those days very

By living in groups, lionesses are better able to defend their territory and collectively raise their cubs, hunting together and ganging up against outsiders.

few of the camps offered drivers the training programmes that are now mandatory at most camps and lodges.

When the family eventually moved away to another part of their large home range I lost track of them, but in February 1988 a driver from Kichwa Tembo reported that the mother cheetah had been badly injured and separated from her four surviving cubs, who were now eight months old. She had been spotted lying halfway up a stony ridge near Leopard Gorge, a place I used to visit on an almost daily basis in my quest to learn more about leopards. There was blood on the rocks marking where the cheetah had lain, and judging by the tracks a number of vehicles had bounced over the uneven ground to see her, yet inexplicably none had tried to raise help. Nobody is sure how she came to be injured, but the most likely cause was an attack by a lion or a leopard, in which case she was lucky to have escaped with her life. The Wildlife Department was eventually notified and a veterinary surgeon flown to the Mara to

help. But they could find no sign of the injured cheetah. There were only two options: dart the four cubs and take them away to be raised in captivity, or leave them in the wild and feed them – they were too young to survive on their own.

The Senior Warden decided that the most appropriate course of action was to provide the cubs with food, ordering his game rangers to shoot an impala for them whenever necessary. The only problem with this was that without their mother's

Honey carrying a gazelle fawn back to her cubs. When cubs are very young their mother kills prey herself rather than risk losing it while they practise their inexpert hunting skills.

kills. But it takes a long time for a cheetah cub to perfect its hunting skills – they are still inept at the age of ten months – so any lost or abandoned cub younger than this has little choice but to try to join another family in an attempt to parasitize their kills.

At first it might appear as if these intruders are tolerated by the families they latch on to, but closer observation proves otherwise, with mother cheetahs reacting either with indifference or aggressively, slapping and hissing when an 'adopted' cub approaches. Occasionally the foster mother might groom an adoptee, though not as often as she does her own cubs. Her offspring are more tolerant and will sometimes play with the newcomers. An

Kike and one of her nine-month-old cubs play-fighting. Mother cheetahs often join in play sessions and will sometimes discipline cubs if they get too rough, pinning them to the ground without hurting them.

experience in guarding against danger, the cubs might end up sleeping next to a half-eaten carcass – something an adult would never do. Adult cheetahs eat as much as they can from a kill and then move on, distancing themselves from possible conflict with other predators. But somehow the cubs survived, not least because the drivers kept a close eye on them and helped to ensure that predators did not disturb them when they were feeding.

Six weeks later, at the end of March, the cubs disappeared. Much to everyone's surprise, when they were sighted again several months later, there were five of them. Photographic evidence proved that while three of them belonged to the family we had been watching, they had at some point been joined by two males of roughly the same age.

Cats generally live a solitary existence and are intolerant of each other, except when a female is accompanied by cubs. The exceptions to this are, of course, the social lions, but they too act very aggressively towards strangers and it would be unheard of for a pride to accept outsiders into their midst. Cheetah mothers recognize their own cubs by sound and smell, and one would expect them to react in a hostile manner to any attempt by unrelated young to accompany them or to feed from their

Play helps refine hunting and fighting skills, which is particularly important for male cheetahs who as adults may be forced to fight over territory.

RIGHT: Male cheetah descending a boscia tree after sniffing for scent and looking around for prey. Cheetahs regularly climb trees with sloping trunks, but do not rest in them as leopards do.

abandoned cub may even forge a relationship with adult males: researchers in the Serengeti observed a seven-month-old male tagging along with two adult males for at least a month and sharing their kills. The youngster finally lost contact with his companions when they were searching for and then chasing a female. He called repeatedly in his efforts to reunite with them, but was unsuccessful. One of the adult males was observed yipping 20 times around the same time – in the same way that a mother would do if her cubs were lost. This is not as unusual as it might seem. Young males sometimes join forces with unrelated males (as do nomadic lions), and when a singleton allies himself to a group of two brothers, they eventually all act as if they were siblings, resting close together, grooming one another, doing everything possible not to become separated – and calling when they do. A week later the young male was seen 7km (4 miles) away,

having attached himself to a mother and her two grown sons.

Adoptions are not uncommon, and Tim Caro, who took over the Serengeti Cheetah Project from the Frames in 1980 and has written a book called *Cheetahs of the Serengeti Plains*, mentions eleven instances that he and his co-workers witnessed, nine of them involving cubs of six months to a year old and lasting from as little as two days to at least ten months. Youngsters who have managed to link up with another family are quick to follow their foster mother when she moves, and nervous about being left behind. There are no apparent benefits for the foster mother, except perhaps increased protection against predators, but presumably the cost of feeding an extra mouth is insufficient to warrant chasing the cub away or killing it. This tolerance is probably also partly due to the fact that cheetah females are non-territorial and tend to be non-

confrontational by nature. The alternative for the cubs is death by starvation or predation, and the fact that cheetahs do not usually scavenge further limits their options.

Even when Amber's mother and her brothers and adopted brothers were old enough to fend for themselves, the rangers continued to feed them. By this time they were thoroughly habituated to vehicles and people, and regularly climbed up onto bonnets or spare wheels; Amber's mother continued to do this for the rest of her life. One of the males eventually died of abdominal complications – he had already been operated on for the removal of impacted hairballs accumulated from the fur of his prey, which would normally be coughed up. The three surviving males were magnificent animals, considerably larger and heavier than Amber's mother, with the broad head and distinctive ruff of hair that is typical of male cheetahs. For a while after they separated from their sister the three

Nick, the territorial male in the Musiara and Rhino Ridge area during the late 1980s and early 1990s, was a singleton who managed to hold a territory for a number of years, at a time when there were no male coalitions to compete with him. But many of the non-resident singletons I have watched showed none of the confidence that Nick or the Aitong males exhibited, looking ill at ease and acting furtively; if they were anything like their Serengeti counterparts they would have been travelling long distances at night to try to avoid confrontation. This stressful existence means that solitary floaters weigh less and are more likely to suffer ill health than other males, not uncommonly showing signs of mange, a skin condition brought on by infestation with tiny mites that do not cause a problem in healthy individuals. In animals in poor condition, mange can lead to open sores where the animal has scratched itself raw, allowing secondary infections to take hold. In the worst cases the animal dies. In the Serengeti most of the 'floating' males suffer from some sort of infection – ulcerated mouths, gingivitis and poorly healed wounds such as an abscess on the foot, as well as mange. Compared to the residents they also have higher levels of corticosteroids, hormones that are released in greater quantities at times of stress, and raised white blood-cell counts, signs indicating infestation by parasites, stress and general

infections – though some members of the coalitions of floaters show no signs of ill heath. Solitary floaters tend to die about a year earlier than territory holders. In the Serengeti the average lifespan for all adult males was 5.3 years with a maximum of 9.3 years – for females it was 6.2 with a maximum of 13.5. Wild-caught cheetahs living in zoos commonly survive to the age of 12–16 years, with one recorded at 17 years.

Nick, so named because of the nick out of his left ear, was the territorial male in the Rhino Ridge area for a number of years.

Two of the Aitong males investigating scent. They are able to assess whether it was left by a female or a rival male, whether a female was in oestrus and how long ago he or she passed by.

males moved south towards the Talek area, but eventually headed north again to Aitong. This was prime cheetah country, with good concentrations of prey and in those days it supported as high a density of females as anywhere in the Mara, exactly the kind of situation male cheetahs are looking for. As the largest coalition in the area the Aitong males, as they became known, had the freedom to wander where they pleased, in marked contrast to the less confident behaviour of the solitary males we sometimes saw.

Serengeti researchers found that adult male cheetahs either lived alone (40 per cent) or in groups of two (40 per cent) or three (20 per cent). Some 71 per cent of coalitions contained littermates, with most of the pairs being brothers and most of the trios consisting of two brothers who had been joined by a non-relative. The reasons for forming a coalition are clear enough – males will fight over ownership of a territory, and defending yourself is much harder if you are on your own. With such deadly weapons at their disposal, fights can

be lethal. While one member of the coalition challenges an intruder by biting, slapping and attempting to grab him by the throat, his companion – or companions – close in behind their adversary, biting his haunches and genitals. Even if the victim isn't strangled to death, he may well die later of his wounds. Little wonder then that single young males try to make alliances.

Tim Caro feels that singletons form coalitions – or join existing ones – to 'fend off a challenge' or 'set up a territory'. This is most likely to happen towards the end of adolescence or just after it – cheetahs are classed as adolescents from 14–22 months, as young adults from 23–42 months (by which time sibling groups have split up and individuals have achieved adult body weight) and as adults from then onwards. Coalitions are about six times more likely than singletons to claim a territory successfully. But contrary to earlier findings, it seems that once established on a territory, singletons in the Serengeti remain resident for just as long as coalitions, with the average tenure being around four years.

Because female cheetahs do not defend a territory, and on the Serengeti plains roam over huge areas, it is impossible for male cheetahs to adopt the normal cat strategy, whereby an individual attempts to carve out a large territory that overlaps the home ranges of one or more females. Instead the more powerful coalitions of male cheetahs compete for the right to occupy small territories – often less than 5 per cent of the average female home range – known in the Serengeti as 'hot spots'. Hot spots occur in areas where a number of female home ranges overlap, and tend to be clumped, with large distances (and few resident males) separating these clusters. Hot spots typically offer ample concentrations of Thomson's gazelles and good cover for stalking prey and concealing young cubs from the numerous lions and hyenas, with luggas, thickets and kopjes being particularly sought after.

In the Serengeti, hot spots occur at the plains/woodland boundary to which the Thomson's gazelles migrate at the beginning of the dry season. Interestingly, though, female cheetahs do not select the areas with the highest concentrations of gazelles, as these also tend to attract the most lions and hyenas; they prefer intermediate concentrations. The density of female cheetahs at this time of year can be as high as one per 3km^2 (just under one per square mile). In more wooded habitats, such as in parts of southern Africa, cheetahs tend to hunt their prey at the edges of open patches in the woodlands. Here hot spots are more evenly distributed and consequently male territories are not clumped, but border one another and are larger – anything from 60–160km^2 (23–62sq. miles).

In the Serengeti only about 50 per cent of males reaching adolescence survive to old age, which accounts for the predominance of females seen in so many cheetah populations – the sex ratio at birth is 1:1, but in the adult population it is two females for every male. Apart from being killed by a larger predator, the most likely cause of death for adult males is a fight with another cheetah.

The alternative to holding a territory is to be a 'floater' (and all adolescents start out like this), never staying in one area for too long, avoiding the hot spots and territory holders while sneaking as many copulations with oestrus females as they can. This means roaming over huge areas like the females. Some coalitions, not just singletons, adopt this strategy, but even for them floating is probably an enforced way of life – either because there are no unoccupied territories or because they have lost or abandoned their territory – rather than being a deliberate choice yielding greater reproductive success.

Wildebeest and calves. One of these calves was an orphan which had tagged along with the mother and baby, although it would not have been allowed to suckle.

Ted Bailey, who studied leopards in Kruger National Park in South Africa, found that mange was one of the natural checks that kept the leopard population healthy and in balance with its environment. It was more prevalent among dispersing subadults and old animals, and Bailey did not recommend intervention that would simply allow surplus animals to survive and put more pressure on healthy individuals. Better to let nature take its course, he felt.

By comparison to singletons, the Aitong males were a formidable trio and I would sometimes stop to watch them when I drove over to keep track of the pack of wild dogs that ranged over parts of the same area and used to den there. The cheetahs would pause every so often to scent-mark the gardenia bushes and boscia trees, leaving a strong reminder to others in the area that this was their place. And what a sight it was when all three males leapt up onto a fallen tree, defecating on the branches before moving on again. Cheetahs often continue to move in the same direction after investigating prominent scent posts, whereas a puma, for instance,

who detects the scent of another individual immediately leaves the area. Perhaps the reason that cheetahs seem less intimidated by scent is that their low population density means most scent messages are old.

There was an air of menace about the way the Aitong males moved, as if they knew that they were invincible, ready to meet any challenge that other coalitions might bring – for the moment at least. Each of them weighed around 65kg (145lb), as much as most male leopards. But formidable as they must have appeared to another cheetah, they would have been no match for a pack of wild dogs and would have slunk away the moment the Aitong pack crested the horizon – wild dogs have no hesitation in treeing a cheetah or a leopard if they catch it in open country.

I do not know what the eventual fate of the Aitong males was, but I imagine that sooner or later one or more of them was injured in a fight with other males or attacked by lions or a leopard, and died. And when you are old, sick or injured and desperate for food, there are always the hyenas to contend with.

People have for years puzzled over the driving force behind sociality in mammals, identifying food as the primary – though not necessarily the only – reason for it in species such as lions, hyenas and wild dogs. Craig Packer, who has headed the Serengeti Lion Project for the past 20 years, believes that where lionesses live at high densities in open habitats and hunt large prey, they should form groups as a way of trying to prevent scavengers such as vultures and hyenas from stealing their kills; better to share food with relatives and keep the scavengers at bay. Tim Caro maintains that the reason most cats do not form groups is that they typically live in areas where there is not enough large prey available to support a group. But there seems to be a degree of flexibility inherent in cat behaviour that would allow them to adapt to an altered environment.

This is borne out by the way domestic cats readily form groups where sufficient food is available to them. In one study, cats at a dockyard site lived in family groups of four to five females, while those living on a farm gave birth in communal dens, formed

Two male cheetahs capturing a wildebeest calf in the Ngorongoro Crater. Members of male coalitions can kill animals up to the size of adult female zebras and yearling wildebeest.

A Cheetah called Amber 77

nursing coalitions and jointly defended kittens against infanticidal males, just as lionesses do. Over time, the female domestic cats formed subgroups of friendly, tightly knit clans made up of several generations of relatives descended from the same mother. As with the lionesses in a pride, a matriline is the basic social unit of group-living domestic cats. Tigresses in Chitwan in Nepal live in overlapping home ranges that are often shared by sisters, mothers and aunts, and it is possible that under certain circumstances it would make sense for these related females to form a pride – perhaps if the habitat was more open and there was more intense competition from vultures, hyenas and other scavengers.

Even the highly specialized, fragile-looking cheetah could no doubt adapt its ways to a changed environment, and in some ways its lifestyle, featuring solitary females and males living alone or in coalitions, reveals a degree of flexibility not seen in any of the other carnivores.

Though coalitions of males are better fed than singletons because they need to take larger prey such as wildebeest, there is little active co-operation when hunting and in most instances it is a single male who makes the kill. Having a partner may make it easier to thwart a cow wildebeest or topi mother's efforts to defend her calf, and in some instances the added strength helps the cheetahs to overpower large prey. But the real benefits of a coalition seem to lie in being better able to hold a prime territory and thus to increase the chances of mating.

Like the Aitong males, Amber's mother proved to be something of a legend and raised a number of cubs to maturity. As an adult, Amber shared a large part of her natal range with her mother. And like most cheetahs in the Mara her home range was so large that she inevitably spent part of her time outside the reserve. Though the area beyond the boundary suited Amber well enough, and meant that she was less likely

to be bothered by lions and hyenas, there was always the risk posed by poachers.

Meat poaching has been a problem in the Mara for as long as I can remember – and not just inside the reserve. As the human population has swelled around the shores of Lake Victoria to the west, the land has been subdivided and then subdivided again, forcing people to disperse towards the fertile lands surrounding the Mara. Although the Masai traditionally shun the meat of wild animals unless stricken by drought, the chance of a free meal or a quick profit from killing wild animals is well established among other ethnic groups. The poaching gangs set hundreds of wire snares in and around the reserve, retreating each day to camps hidden in the forest shrouding the Mara River or deep within dense patches of bush and forests along the Siria Escarpment.

Wire snares are cheap and indiscriminate weapons of destruction, and there is always the danger that a predator might get tangled up in one and die. This happened to Half-Tail in early 1999 after she took a sheep or goat, and a snare was concealed in the wall of the cattle boma that she had managed to squeeze through. Warren Samuels, who has gained a reputation as an outstanding wildlife cameraman with a particular affinity for big cats – cheetahs are his speciality – witnessed Amber being caught up in a snare one afternoon in March 1998. Fortunately he was close at hand to release her. This was not the first time she had run into trouble with poachers – Jomo, the head driver at Governor's Camp, had freed her from a snare once before.

Warren had found Amber at first light and watched as she entertained a succession of vehicles by clambering all over them. By the middle of the day the last of the vehicles had long since returned to camp, and Warren and his crew looked forward to spending some quality time with the cheetahs. Amber had three one-year-old cubs, the same cubs that we filmed later

that year during the second series of *Big Cat Diary*. Warren had watched from a distance as Amber got up, stretched and then led the cubs away in search of food. When the cubs emerged from a lugga without their mother, Warren knew instinctively that something was amiss. He drove forward to investigate and to his horror found Amber cartwheeling in the air in a frantic attempt to free herself from a snare. But all she succeeded in doing was pulling the wire noose tighter around her throat. Her large amber eyes bulged from their sockets, her tongue began to turn blue and froth drooled from her nose and lips. There wasn't a moment to lose if they were to save her.

The three cubs stood looking confused, not sure what was happening, then ran off as Warren and his crew jumped from the camera vehicle to help their mother. They grabbed a tarpaulin and threw it over the panic-stricken cat. Instantly she calmed down and stopped struggling – a minute longer and she would have suffocated. While one man held the tarpaulin over Amber's legs to stop her scratching him, another cut the wire from its anchor around the base of an acacia tree using a *panga* or machete, then loosened the noose from around her throat. The men lifted Amber gently to her feet. She staggered away a few metres and then lay down, exhausted.

Thirty minutes later she emerged from the lugga and the cubs ran to greet her, licking at her face. Warren walked down the lugga towards the river. Every 15–20m (50–65ft) he found a large snare, hugging the path taken by animals as they trekked each day to the life-giving water. Kipsegis hunters had set the snares to catch zebras. The moon was ripe and men would have crept among the shadows at night, butchering whatever had been caught and moving it out – on foot, by bicycle or on donkeys. If they had found Amber before the hyenas did, they might have taken her pelt to make a rug or adornment, and cut

Two of Kike's nine-month-old cubs playing on the spare wheel
and the roof of one of our camera cars.

the dewclaws from her forepaws to use as ornaments for a necklace. But it was meat these hunters were after, not skins. At that time tonnes of dried meat were being spirited away to destinations as far afield as Lake Victoria and Uganda.

Amber was least successful as a mother when she tried raising her cubs inside the reserve, where the chances of them being killed by predators was greater. The Marsh Lions certainly accounted for one of her litters, possibly two, and she lost another when the cubs were two or three weeks old, after a herd of buffaloes stampeded through the long grass bordering the Bila Shaka Lugga. The two cubs were concealed among a tussock in a hollow in the ground, and when vehicles out on a game drive unwittingly disturbed the buffaloes, they sent a groundswell of massive bodies surging across the grasslands and through the thickets, crashing and grunting as they went. One of the cubs was killed instantly, the other was later abandoned. A single surviving cub is likely to starve sooner or later, because it cannot suckle enough to stimulate its mother's milk supply. Harsh as it may seem, abandoning the cub was the right decision. Within a few weeks Amber was pregnant again, and three of her new litter survived to maturity.

Kike's Story

Amber disappeared in March 2002. Nobody is sure how old she was, but she would have done well to survive to eight or nine years. She might even have reached the ripe old age of twelve, which for a solitary big cat in the wild would be remarkable and would equal Half-Tail's age when her life was brought to an abrupt end (a leopard could be considered old at ten). Amber's legacy is Kike, the cheetah who has taken the habit of climbing on cars to a completely new level, and she is as unique to us as her leopard counterpart Zawadi. Big cats such as these bring joy to all who are lucky enough to spend time in their company, and they are truly remarkable in the way that they accommodate our daily intrusion into their lives.

Angie and I never knew Kike as a cub; we were too busy following Half-Tail to venture as far afield as Aitong Hill and the Talek River where she grew up in the late 1990s. By all accounts she is now about six years old and she is certainly as beautiful a cheetah as you could hope to find, of average weight – perhaps 40kg (90lb) – with none of the signs of mange along the edges of her ears that often appear among cheetahs who are old or beginning to lose condition.

She would have conceived for the first time at some point during her third year, approximately a year after she left her mother and six months after splitting up from any siblings. We do know that the cubs we filmed for *Big Cat Week* were born around the middle of December 2002. Our friend Paul Goldstein, who is co-owner of Kicheche Mara Camp, situated not far from Aitong, photographed Kike on 23 December, watching as she moved four tiny cubs to a new den site 100m (330ft) away. The cubs' eyes were still tightly closed and the round black spots so typical of a cheetah's coat markings were masked by the darkness of their belly fur; their backs were covered in a mantle of long, silvery-white hair. When Paul first saw Kike she was with the cubs in long grass about 400m

Kike – as beautiful a cheetah as you could hope to find, and a delight to filmmakers and tourists alike.

(1,300ft) from the southern corner of the Bila Shaka Lugga, the same spot that the Marsh Lions so often favour as the birthplace for their cubs. Typically, Kike jumped onto the bonnet of Paul's vehicle and then tried to climb onto the roof.

To prevent drivers from criss-crossing the area of long grass where Kike had hidden her cubs, the Kenya Wildlife Service and Governor's Camp closed off the area surrounding the den. The short rains had been particularly heavy and the Mara's poorly drained black-cotton soils would quickly have churned the area into a muddy

morass as vehicles competed with one another to catch a glimpse of newborn cubs. In 2000 Angie and I had seen for ourselves just how close tour vehicles will approach, moving to within 1m (3ft) of a dense patch of bush that a mother cheetah had chosen for her den in the Mara Triangle – the grass had been flattened by a succession of vehicles and we were worried that one or more of the cubs might end up under the wheels of a car. Some females are so habituated to vehicles that they can withstand this kind of pressure, but most have no option but to move their cubs to a

Spotted hyena cubs at a den. The normal litter size is two, sometimes three. Their natal coat is black, the spotted pattern emerging by the time they are four months old.

new location, sometimes with disastrous consequences. When we returned to the Triangle the following day there was no sign of either mother or cubs, and the next time we saw the female she had evidently lost or abandoned her litter.

Now we were concerned that the heavy rain might cause a flash flood along the lugga and that Kike's cubs would drown or die of exposure, as had happened to a litter that another cheetah had hidden here many years earlier. But as always it was the lions and hyenas that we were most concerned about.

It is hard to understand why lions show such antipathy towards other predators – not just other cats; they are also one of the biggest threats to wild dog puppies once they leave the safety of their underground den and start to follow the pack. Male lions seem particularly despotic in this regard – I had seen one kill a hyena cub at a den along the Bila Shaka Lugga in the 1970s, close to where Kike now had her cubs. He was one of two nomadic lions whom I had been following for some months and who eventually managed to take over the Marsh Pride's territory. He had caught sight of the two tiny black-coated hyena cubs playing at the entrance to their den while their mother was off on some errand – hunting,

perhaps, or patrolling her clan territory. The male was on his way back to the lugga, already heavy with food and ready to lie up for the rest of the day until the heat drained from the plains. But the sight of the cubs scampering about caught his attention. His expression changed instantly. No longer did he hang his head, mouth half-open. His eyes narrowed and his jaw tightened into an aggressive mien. He trotted, then slunk towards the cubs, accelerating as he closed the gap, timing his final rush to perfection and pouncing on one of the terrified youngsters. He bit down on the cub's neck, immediately stifling its cries of pain. He strutted around with the tiny corpse hanging from his jaws. Then just as quickly he dropped it, grimacing as he sucked in the scent of the hyena, wrinkling his nose and curling his lip in a flehmen face. And then he walked away.

I was relatively new to Africa and at the time felt outraged at the apparent wantonness of the killing. It seemed so gratuitous, so wasteful; the snuffing out of a life for what? This wasn't killing for food: I might have felt better if the lion had at least eaten his little victim, though I had no doubt that any hyena – not least the cub's mother – would devour it. Later I was able to see the killing as part of the balance between predators, the playing out of the hierarchy that gives order to life on the plains and among the thorn thickets. This was competition at its most brutal and basic. There are three times as many spotted hyenas in the Mara as there are lions – 1,500 compared to 500 – and the fact that lions sometimes kill hyenas – and wild dogs, leopards and cheetahs – is nature's way of placing checks and balances on their numbers.

In April 2003 I had my first opportunity really to get to know Kike – until now she had just been a name that I had heard much of from the drivers and guides (though they called her Princess – daughter of Queen). I was due to stay for a

few days at Mara Intrepids, a tented camp hidden away among riverine forest along the Talek River, the same location where we filmed Bella the leopard with two cubs later that year. It felt strange to be watching a cheetah female in this area again, as this was where Angie and I had followed another of Amber's daughters three years earlier – one of the three cubs that we had filmed with their mother in 1998. By then she had left her two brothers and a few months later gave birth to her first litter. Angie spent days at a time trying to track her down, though when she next appeared it was apparent that she had lost her cubs. But we did manage to find her again while filming the *Big Cat Diary* update in 1999.

At that time this young female was the only one in the area – apart from her mother – who regularly jumped onto vehicles. We found her wandering around an old murram pit where earth had been dug out to help service the dilapidated road leading from Musiara Gate to the reserve headquarters at Sekenani, on the other side of the reserve. I had seen her here before; it was one of those places in a cheetah's home range that they always visit when passing through, a place to sniff around for signs of what other cheetahs have been doing. Nick, the territorial male who had probably sired the female's first litter, always deviated on his travels to spend time here, invariably climbing onto one of the large slabs of rock that surround the shallow pool of water in the abandoned murram pit, depositing his calling card in the form of faeces, so that other cheetahs would know that the area was occupied. He occasionally stopped long enough to slake his thirst from the muddy water, though like all of Africa's big cats he could go without drinking when necessary.

The murram pit was situated on a high point, providing an unimpeded view across the rolling plains towards Mara Intrepids, and there were always lots of Thomson's gazelles in the area for Nick to hunt. He was a large male, with a telltale nick out of his right ear, hence his name, and he probably weighed around 50–60kg (110–130lb), putting him near the top of the cheetah's weight range.

At some point between 2000 and 2002 Amber's daughter disappeared. She had looked in poor health when we last filmed her having a scrap with Nick in 2000, and may simply have died. If not, she must have moved away from the area where we used to find her, establishing herself in a new home range – and that seemed unlikely. But if we were all sad to see her go, Kike quickly stole our hearts.

For female cheetahs to lead a successful life they must establish a home range that can provide adequate food for themselves and their cubs. By the time a young female becomes independent, she will have gained a good understanding of the seasonal movements of prey throughout the area she has roamed with her mother, as well as learning the best places to find shade, safe hiding places and water. The high mortality of cheetah cubs unwittingly ensures that there is ample room for the survivors in places like the Mara–Serengeti.

Kike's litter consisted of a male and two females, and Angie quickly noticed that one of the females was much more timid and nervous than her sister and brother. She was the first to follow Kike when she started to move away, as if unduly worried about being left behind; she certainly seemed less carefree than her siblings; and whenever danger threatened she was generally the first to bolt – a similar temperament to Safi, Zawadi's daughter. By the time we started filming *Big Cat Week* the cubs were eight and a half months old and already capable of climbing onto the spare wheels on the back of my car.

During filming, the search for Kike and her cubs would begin before dawn. After a few days the routine would become as predictable as clockwork – no need for a wake-up call at 5 a.m.; we would pull on our clothes and grab a quick cup of tea next to the dying embers of the campfire before heading into the darkness, listening to the chatter from our car radios for news of where the other crews were headed. Emerging from the shroud of forest that

Kike play-fighting with her nine-month-old male club. The three cubs would often play first thing in the morning while it was cool, though as they got older they played less frequently.

Kike's movement around her home range seemed to be primarily motivated by where she could find food; this was determined to a large extent by the seasonal movement of the Thomson's gazelles, and initially at least she concentrated most of her efforts on hunting gazelle fawns. There were times when she was very localized in her movements and might spend two weeks or more in a particular area, either because there was plenty for her to hunt or because there was less competition from other predators. She also responded to seasonal peaks in the birth of various prey animals that she never killed as adults – young topis, Coke's hartebeest and warthogs all featured in her diet. When the migration moved into the Mara in June and July, she also preyed on wildebeest calves (born the previous February) – or tried to – and targeted the topi calves and warthog piglets the minute they appeared in September and October, just before the onset of the short rains. There were a number of male cheetahs – but no coalitions – in Kike's area, and during the dry season they always seemed to be on the look-out for wildebeest calves whenever they were searching for prey.

Kike chasing a warthog piglet. Groups of male cheetahs occasionally prey on adult warthogs, but a mother cheetah must not take unnecessary risks; if she is injured and unable to hunt, her cubs are doomed.

marks the Mara River, we would rejoice in the red and orange colours of the dawn, hoping to find our quarry before the first golden glimmer of light peeped above the horizon – the perfect time for photography. Some mornings we would find the cheetahs already feeding on a kill. But if there was a chill wind, then as often as not Kike and the cubs would still be huddled together in the long grass along Rhino Ridge. Sometimes they wedged themselves among the rocks, shielded from the frosty morning air by the boulders that litter the flanks of the ridge, the cubs staring in fascination at the giant silhouette of a giraffe or elephant against a pale morning sky, waiting for the warming rays of sunlight to thaw the cold from their lean bodies.

During 36 days of observation we saw Kike hunt successfully on all but four days, and we suspected that there were times when she hunted as it got dark. Rain or overcast skies often prompted her to go in search of food, taking advantage of the fact that gazelles and other antelopes tended to hunch up with their backs to the wind and become less vigilant. Gazelle fawns were by far her most important source of food; she killed 34 of them during this period. On 14 occasions she took more than one a day, once managing to catch three within two hours between 7 and 9 a.m. She also killed one adult male and four adult female gazelles during this period. She hunted topi calves five times and always caught them, but on three of these occasions she was forced to drop the calf when the topi mother turned and charged her, bellowing with aggression. This would have been the outcome on a fourth occasion, too, if vehicles hadn't crowded in around Kike so quickly that the mother was intimidated from attempting to rescue her calf.

Kike contesting ownership of a hare she has just killed with her nine-month-old cubs. This was one of the rare occasions when she seemed determined to get something to eat herself.

Cheetahs, wild dogs, leopards and occasionally lions all target impalas. For the antelopes, being part of a herd helps lessen the risk of predation – there are more eyes and ears to detect danger.

Kike's largest meal was a female reedbuck. She also killed a young Grant's gazelle, an impala fawn, a hare and two warthog piglets, and was forced to release a third piglet unharmed when its mother charged in. She chased and missed an oribi and made a number of unsuccessful attempts to catch wildebeest calves, invariably being thwarted by the mother's determined defence. Besides these animals, on four occasions she captured Thomson's gazelle fawns that were subsequently taken by hyenas – in three instances this happened when she released the fawns to her cubs for them to practise their hunting skills and hyenas spotted them running around. The fourth time, the cheetahs had virtually finished eating the fawn when a hyena rushed in and stole the leg bones and skin.

Of the 51 kills or captures we witnessed, Kike lost only three complete kills and the one she had partly eaten to hyenas. This represents a loss of 6 per cent to hyenas. In addition she lost one kill (2 per cent) to lions – not as much as one might have expected, which highlights the effectiveness of hunting in the heat of the day when these other predators are less active.

It is interesting to compare these findings with how Zawadi behaved when she had cubs, though there were times when she killed and ate prey during the

night that we were unable to account for. Like Kike, Zawadi took advantage of seasonal changes in prey availability, targeting young impalas whenever she could, and during one ten-day period she killed four warthog piglets, once taking two in a single day. Over the course of 42 days she killed two dik-diks, four warthog piglets, five impala fawns, one waterbuck calf, one topi calf and one wildebeest calf – young animals that were relatively easy for her to catch during daytime and most of which she ate on the ground. She also took an adult male and an adult female Thomson's gazelle and an adult female impala – all more difficult to catch, all taken at night and all carried into trees. Zawadi hunted more often during the daytime when she had small cubs, perhaps to avoid competition with lions and hyenas, and she often carried small kills back to the cubs once they were two to three months old. She didn't have to hunt as often as Kike and was more adaptable. The fact that leopards can hunt a wide variety of prey day and night, often manage to hoist their kills safely into trees to feed on them at leisure and will scavenge from animals that have died or been killed by other predators, highlights just how specialized a cheetah is by comparison.

Just as Zawadi targeted young impalas, so Kike harvested gazelle fawns on a daily basis for as long as they were plentiful – and Thomson's gazelles experience a birth peak around the times of the long and short rains. Kike's success rate was almost 100 per cent. Her tactics were simple. She would scan the plains for a herd of gazelles and watch until she saw a youngster. This might be when a mother came back to the place where her fawn had been lying with its chin to the ground in a posture of concealment, patiently waiting for its mother to stop grazing and return to suckle

it. The fawn would often choose a shallow depression or tuft of long grass among the plains that were otherwise chewed to stubble, offering a touch more cover than the shortest grass.

Spotting such a fawn, Kike's ears would prick up and then she would be off, either stalking quickly towards it, to get as close as possible before breaking into an easy run, or not even bothering to stalk. Her long strides would eat up the ground, lengthening and quickening as the gazelles sensed the danger and scattered like a shoal

Female leopard strangling a male impala – a sizeable animal weighing considerably more than the predator.

If the family had fed the previous evening the cubs would either be comatose or in playful mood, haring after one another, tumbling and pirouetting, playing a cheetah's version of 'I'm the king of the castle', enticing each other to join in the fun. Much of their play had elements of the hunt – stalking, grabbing each other's rump, rearing up and reaching over their shoulders with their forepaws – 'riding' their 'victim' – wrestling their playmate to the ground and biting at the throat. Sometimes Kike would join in, but it was never long before her attention turned to the endless quest to feed her cubs.

of fish fleeing from a shark, some of them performing the stiff-legged bouncing strut known as stotting, pronking or spronking. This attention-seeking display is a way for gazelles to show off their fitness and lack of vulnerability to a cheetah or hunting dog, in essence saying, 'I have seen you, look at me run, you can't catch me, so give up now and stop wasting both of our time.' Fawns sometimes do this, too, though in their case it may be a way of letting their mother know they have moved or simply of exercising young muscles.

Invariably Kike would overtake the fawn, though some of the older ones made her work a bit harder for her meal, performing breakneck turns and zigzagging each time Kike closed the gap, momentarily gaining a metre or two. By cornering sharply like this the gazelle forced Kike to follow and in the process slowed her down. Every second that the chase continued worked to the gazelle's advantage – but only in the case of these older fawns or adults. Adult gazelles have more endurance than a cheetah and not uncommonly manage to outdistance their pursuer, who after a few hundred metres must abandon the chase. Kike would signal defeat by flexing her long tail high in the air, like a white flag of surrender, pulling abruptly to a halt in a cloud of dust, then either retracing her steps to where her cubs were waiting or lying down to recover her breath, panting so rapidly that it was impossible to count the beats.

The same technique is employed by all cats and was Kike's way of cooling herself down, synchronizing her panting and breathing to the same rhythm. Cats have very few sweat glands, except on their feet, so this method of cooling evaporates moisture from the vascular mucous membranes of their tongue and mouth, lowering the blood temperature that reaches a critical level in prolonged high-speed chases. But it costs moisture that must be replenished either by drinking from pools of rainwater or streams, or by lapping up the blood and body fluids of prey. In arid areas cheetahs confine their hunting activities to the coolest part of the

Kike chasing a Thomson's gazelle fawn. Her success rate in capturing young fawns was almost 100 per cent.

day – the early morning, late evening or night – as a way of conserving water and energy, and they can live entirely without drinking water for long periods of time. But in the Mara, where water is generally available even in the dry season, Kike would often lead her cubs down to one of the luggas to drink after eating or if they had been forced to lie for long periods in the open.

Once a mother gazelle realized that a predator was hurtling towards her, her only defence was to run, perhaps hoping to draw the cheetah's attention away from her baby. More often than not there was no escape once Kike had a fawn in her sights; she would hunt it down, ignoring any adults fleeing around her, proving time and again that she was the fastest thing on four feet in a one-on-one race. Once she had bowled her prey over, tripping it with outstretched paw and snagging it with her dewclaw, the end was inevitable. Sometimes the fawn would follow its mother's lead and race after her or it would lie down, hiding its conspicuous white belly from view in the hope that its tawny

Two of Kike's nine-month-old cubs manhandling a gazelle fawn their mother has released to them. By this age cubs are learning to apply a killing bite to the throat of their victim.

upper body would merge sufficiently with the colours of warm earth and yellow grass to evade detection.

When this happened – or sometimes just as a way of scouring the plains for such hidden fawns – Kike would slow to a deliberate walk, keeping her eyes firmly fixed on the spot where the youngster had

settled. Very occasionally she would fail to relocate her victim, but nine times out of ten she walked right up to it, standing over it and marking the place until the cubs arrived, then dabbed at the fawn with her forepaw to force it to its feet, at which point the cubs would chase, trip and knock the baby flying, biting and mouthing its head and throat in a protracted game of touch and release. This might go on for as much as 20 minutes, with the tiny fawn becoming increasingly weary and dishevelled, its bleats of distress growing fainter, its coat sodden from the cubs' saliva.

Just occasionally a fawn would outrun the cubs or they would lose interest, particularly when their mother first released prey to them when they were four to five months old, but this was rare – Kike always kept a watchful eye on their bungling attempts to subdue the fawn. At the first sign that it might escape (it happened just once while we were watching), she would run it down again, dispatching it quickly with a throat hold and allowing the cubs to feed. But mostly she held back, walking around like a match official, stemming her own desire to eat for the sake of the cubs' development, making sure the prey (and potentially her own meal) didn't elude her

The cubs' practice hunting sessions may go on for ten minutes or more without them killing the prey. At this point their mother is likely to step in again so that they can all eat.

The hours from 11 a.m. to 4 p.m. were the worst, time suspended and hanging like the gallows. Gone was the lovely light for photography; the playful cubs lay flat as pancakes, drained of all energy. Wildebeest and zebras would stand as if stunned by the heat, senses numbed. This was when I stared into the depths of my picnic bag for inspiration or rummaged around the car in the hope of finding a secret trove of some special treat – nuts or biscuits, a packet of crisps or bar of chocolate. Week-old

newspapers would be scanned yet again for a missed article, the hands of my wristwatch never seeming to move. And then finally, almost imperceptibly, four o'clock came and the temperature dropped a degree or two. By five o'clock the light was beginning to turn golden and by six the colours were warm and rich. I could breathe again and I longed for Kike and the cubs to emerge from their resting place and pose on a termite mound or fallen tree.

offspring and keeping watch for potential danger – lions and hyenas could easily surprise the cubs while they were so engrossed with the fawn.

Kike's concerns were well founded. On a number of occasions hyenas spotted the tell-tale signs of another predator at work – gazelles fleeing across the plains or alarm-calling, animals running or standing alert, vultures circling overhead – and ran to investigate, rushing in to snatch the fawn from under the cubs' noses. Though there was nothing that Kike could do to prevent the inexperienced cubs losing their meal, she could at least ensure that they did not get hurt, confronting a hyena with hackles raised to make herself look more intimidating, hissing or uttering a low moaning growl, even at times charging forward and slapping the hyena on the rump or biting it, before darting away again to avoid any reprisals from her larger adversary.

Following Kike and her cubs meant spending 14 to 15 hours each day in the car without a scrap of shade. This was taxing, even to someone like me who always maintains that watching wild creatures in their natural environment is not a question of possessing inexhaustible patience, but simply of doing what I love most. Quite often, when a patch of shade presented itself in the form of a croton thicket on an otherwise open hillside or a cluster of long grass, Kike and the cubs would spend the middle hours of the day resting, leaving me isolated in my tin box, which became like an oven, soaking up the heat. Worst of all

was when the atmosphere was still and heavy; I would long for the slightest breath of cool air. But in the dry season there were days when the sun rolled across clear blue skies, playing hide and seek with voluminous clouds that always threatened rain but refused to deliver it.

As Kike's cubs grew larger she had to work harder to feed them, either by increasing the number of gazelle fawns she killed or by targeting adult gazelles and the young of larger species. Increasingly she attempted to ambush wildebeest calves from among the massed herds, picking out a straggler whenever she could, particularly when they were moving through long grass, making it more difficult for the cows to defend their young.

One morning at first light, Angie found Kike close to where we had left her the previous evening. She was huddled with the cubs in the long golden grass – three little faces poking over their mother's long back. The night sky had been aglow with stars, illuminated by a half-moon. The stormy cloudscape of the previous day had vanished. Now the sun burst above the horizon, dusting the grass heads with gold. The cubs began to play, running circles around Kike as she climbed up onto a termite mound at the base of a beautiful boscia tree. Up here on a high point along Rhino Ridge it was like being on top of the world. To the east Kike could see the Mara Intrepids airstrip running parallel to the Talek River, an area she often hunted, where the grass was always short and there were plenty of gazelles. Directly in front of

her the Topi Plains rolled all the way down to Musiara Marsh, and to the south lay the Paradise Plain, which she also occasionally visited.

As the sun rose quickly into the sky, a herd of wildebeest moved from the high ground where they had spent the night to feed on the plains below, passing down and across the ridge in full view of Kike. She immediately began to stalk and then broke into a trot, quickly closing the gap. The wildebeest started to run, cutting a path through the long grass, prompting Kike to accelerate, scattering the herd, looking for the young calf that she had spotted in their midst, born late in the calving season and now pressed like a limpet to its mother's side as they galloped away. She charged after them with a blinding burst of speed and in a flash wrestled the calf to the ground, disappearing with it in a blanket of long grass. The herd continued on its way, almost as if it had not even noticed that the calf had been taken.

Kike's tactics had been perfect. The wildebeest, including the calf's mother, had been thrown into total disarray. Unsure what was attacking them in the long grass when the first animal bolted, they had stampeded; in fact there was so much confusion, with animals running in every direction, that we didn't even see Kike grab the calf – it was off its feet within seconds. The three cubs had followed their mother's lead, rushing this way and that, chasing the wildebeest through the long grass, inadvertently adding to the mayhem and distracting the adults.

Kike stood up, releasing her hold on the calf's throat. She looked around for the cubs, which had briefly lost sight of her when she charged into the herd. She yipped and they ran to her. By now the calf had regained consciousness and the male cub immediately grabbed it by the throat, pinning it to the ground. The female cubs seemed more nervous than their larger brother, confused by the flailing hooves that bicycled through the air like a threshing machine, clouting one of them in the face as it desperately fought to get back on its feet. At one point it managed to do so, and the little female pulled back, looking perplexed, not sure how to react. Meanwhile her sister joined their brother in holding onto the calf, but the thick mane of hair around its throat made it difficult for them to subdue it and the calf started to bawl in distress.

Kike was ravenous. As far as we could tell she had eaten nothing for the past 36 to 48 hours, and her waist was even more wasp-like than usual. While the cubs held the calf down and strangled it, she quickly began to open up the abdomen, shearing through the thin skin along the edge of the belly nearest to the groin with her carnassial teeth. There was no time to waste. The previous evening she had been disturbed by hyenas while resting on a termite mound with the cubs and knew that at any moment her competitors might come rushing over the horizon to rob her of her hard-earned meal. But this time it was lions she to contend with. Two lionesses, their stomachs swollen with meat from their own kill, had heard the calf's forlorn bleats. They instantly recognized that another predator was active in the heart of their territory and were determined to claim whatever was being killed. Proceeding cautiously at first so as to not give themselves away in case it was other lions (two lionesses might not be enough to challenge intruders, which is why lionesses so often travel in numbers), they stalked through the long grass, their faces frozen in a menacing, poker-faced scowl. Once they were certain that it wasn't lions but a smaller cat, they rushed forward.

Fortunately, at that moment Kike sat up to look round. Seeing the lions, she lowered her head and uttered a low moan of warning to her cubs, who immediately scattered, not even stopping to see what the danger was. Kike held her ground until the last moment, then veered off, drawing the first lioness after her. The second lioness charged straight past the kill, intent on running down the cubs, and at one point

Kike struggling to overpower an eight-month-old wildebeest calf. This is about the largest prey that a female cheetah can tackle.

A few minutes after this photograph was taken, two lionesses stole the kill before the cheetahs could eat. Kike was most successful when she hunted smaller prey such as gazelles.

Kike looking down towards Paradise Plain with the Siria Escarpment in the background.
She often became more active when it was cool and overcast or when it rained.

looked as if she might manage to do so as one of them popped up out of the grass to see what was happening. The lionesses were frighteningly persistent, harrying the cubs and showing a surprising turn of speed and endurance. But the cubs were too quick and eventually the lionesses turned and made their way back to the kill.

Once the immediate panic was over, Kike began to search for the cubs, climbing up out of the long grass onto the termite mounds and calling repeatedly until they were all reunited.

During the months that Angie and I followed Kike and her cubs, we always kept an eye out for other cheetahs in the area. We already knew of one large, rather battered-looking territorial male who overlapped part of Kike's home range, and two other younger males whom we saw occasionally. Both these youngsters were much more nervous than the old male and avoided climbing onto termite mounds or fallen trees which might have made them conspicuous to other males, provoking conflict. Neither of them scent-marked as far as we could tell. The only other cheetah we saw on a regular basis was a young female who, we later discovered from our photographs, was the one who had given birth to four cubs on the Bila Shaka Lugga in July 2002 – and whose cubs had been killed by one of the Marsh Pride. We wondered whether the two females were related, but had no way of telling.

This young female was pregnant during the filming of *Big Cat Week* and, like Kike, preyed heavily on gazelle fawns. In fact the two females were often within view of each other and would stare alertly at each other from 1km (½ mile) or more, their distinctive silhouettes standing out against the skyline, with Kike growling loudly enough for her cubs to know that something was amiss. It is rare for adult females to interact – most of the time they simply wander off in different directions and this was generally what happened with Kike and the young female, though neither seemed keen to

leave the area around Rhino Ridge that for the month of September was covered with gazelle fawns. On one occasion, however, the young female simply sat and watched as Kike moved in her direction and, when Kike suddenly took off after a gazelle fawn, briefly trotted after her, making us wonder if we might soon see a confrontation.

Finally the showdown that had been brewing happened. To our surprise, it was the young female who decided to walk straight towards Kike after each of them had stared at the other for about half an hour. As the young female drew closer, her hackles slightly raised, half stalking now, Kike appeared more and more nervous, growling softly and looking back over her shoulder. The cubs had disappeared under Angie's car. I felt sure that as a mother Kike would chase the young female away. Instead it was the young female who ran the last few metres to face off with Kike, but pulled up short and yipped as Kike gave way. There was no contact, no snarling, not even a real show of aggression on the part of either cat – it was all very low key. When the cubs ran from under the car in response to growls from the young female, Kike made sure she kept between them and her adversary, and the other female then slunk away. But a message was passed nonetheless, perhaps because the young female was about to give birth and wanted to be left alone. By the following morning Kike and the cubs had moved away from Rhino Ridge.

We had hoped that the young female might have her cubs while we were still filming, but our luck had run out. When she gave birth a week or so later, she again chose the Bila Shaka area – and paid the price. The cubs never emerged from the den, reminding us just how difficult it is for a cheetah to raise cubs in an area like this. So far Kike had defied all predictions.

Namibia: Cheetah Capital of the World

When Angie and I started working on this series of books on Africa's big cats in 2001, we were determined to extend the focus beyond East Africa. The findings of the Serengeti Wildlife Research Centre (SWRC) – formerly the Serengeti Research Institute (SRI) – have had such a powerful influence on the way we view Africa's large predators, be they lions, hyenas, wild dogs or cheetahs, that it has sometimes seemed as if the story of their lives were complete. The first wave of full-time scientists arrived in the 1960s, drawn from around the world by the chance to study in the Serengeti, investigating every aspect of the ecosystem – biology, soils, geology, climate – in an effort to gain a sound enough understanding of how the system worked to be able to advise on its conservation.

Unless you know how many animals there are, and understand their patterns of behaviour, how can you conserve them effectively? As always, the large predators tended to steal the limelight, and the Serengeti lion and cheetah projects continue to this day, with scientists at SWRC able to trace family histories back to great-grandparents of present-day cats.

But as research gathered pace in southern Africa, particularly in the Kruger National Park and the Okavango Delta, it became apparent that the Mara–Serengeti was only part of the story. Predators possess considerable flexibility in their behaviour, moulding themselves to their environment: in wooded habitats or dryer regions they sometimes adopt very different strategies in order to survive. This

was why Angie and I wanted to gain a broader view than could be provided by our old stamping grounds.

For this book, our primary destination was Namibia, a country that has become known as the cheetah capital of the world.

Sunrise at Palmwag Rhino Camp.

View near Sera Cafema Camp, on the Kunene River. Namibia's starkly beautiful desert landscape is home to the oryx or gemsbok, as it is known in southern Africa.

Namibia: Cheetah Capital of the World 93

In particular we wanted to spend time with two remarkable women – Laurie Marker of the Cheetah Conservation Fund (CCF) and Lise Hanssen of the AfriCat Foundation – who have done more to raise awareness of the plight of the cheetah than anyone else.

Though the Mara–Serengeti is home to the largest population of cheetahs living within a protected area, it came as a surprise to most people when it emerged that Namibia, one of the most atypical of African countries with its magellanic penguins and desert elephants, had almost six times as many. But although juvenile mortality among cheetahs is low here due to the eradication of most of the large predators, the adults suffer high mortality through persecution by man – potentially a serious problem for the long-term viability of the population, as it is the breeding animals that are suffering the most.

Namibia is a starkly beautiful, parched land: 16 per cent of it is true desert, 49 per cent is classified as arid and 32 per cent as semi-arid, and the climate oscillates wildly between wet and dry spells, with droughts lasting regularly from four to nine years and the most recent one continuing from 1979 to 1995. Despite these harsh conditions, the vast majority of Namibia's sparse population depends on some form of agriculture or livestock farming to sustain them. By a strange quirk of circumstances Namibia now finds itself custodian to nearly a quarter of the world's cheetahs, with 95 per cent of them – and 70 per cent of Namibia's wildlife – roaming the 6,000 commercial livestock ranches that produce cattle, sheep and goats, and in some cases, as we shall see, earn a better living by utilizing the wildlife on their land for profit

For most of its recent history, Namibia was known as South-West Africa, controlled and administered as part of South Africa, with all the odious trappings of apartheid. The largest ranches were owned by descendants of European colonizers, mainly Germans and Afrikaners, who made up only 5 per cent of the population. Namibia won its independence in 1990, but not before the South African Defence Force had played their part in the slaughter of its elephants and rhinos to sell ivory and horn on the international market. Farmers treated predators as vermin, and lions and leopards disappeared from most areas. Today only a few hundred lions survive in protected areas such as Etosha National Park.

I first visited Namibia in 1984 while filming for an American TV series, *Wild Kingdom*. At that time there were an estimated 6,000 cheetahs in Namibia, double the number there are today. The reason for their demise is all too apparent. For many years the cheetah (along with most other predators) were severely persecuted. Not only did farmers view them as a menace to their livestock, there was a

Young cheetah at the Cheetah Conservation Fund's (CCF) headquarters, Otjiwarongo. Where possible cheetahs trapped by farmers are relocated to private game reserves or other suitable areas. Animals too young to hunt for themselves are given a home for life at places such as CCF and the nearby AfriCat Foundation.

price to be earned from trapping them. The decline of East Africa's cheetah population in the 1960s had prompted the passing of laws prohibiting the export of wild cheetahs into captivity, a decision that saw Namibia become the primary source of wild-caught cheetahs for zoos and private individuals. The trade was fuelled by the fact that cheetahs are so difficult to breed in captivity, creating an endless demand for wild-caught animals. Farmers designed traps for this purpose, though they received only a fraction of the value of a live cheetah from game dealers. One such dealer reported selling between 200 and 300 animals each year, 30 to 40 years ago, with a total of over 5,000 animals sold since the 1960s. Prices paid by zoos skyrocketed from US$1,300 in the 1960s to $5,000 in the early 1970s and $6,000 by the early 1980s (king cheetahs fetch anything from $25,000 to $40,000). About 30 per cent of the world's current captive population were caught in Namibia.

Most US and European zoos now exchange cheetahs and co-operate in other ways to improve breeding success. But South Africa, where most of the cheetahs have disappeared from private land into zoos and game parks, has been slow to embrace this initiative. Captive-born cheetah cubs are a valuable commodity and in the past many breeding facilities whose animals had failed to reproduce would ask farmers in Namibia to catch wild ones. This encouraged some farmers to leave their traps open rather than using them only when a problem predator was active on their farm, ignoring the stipulations of the 1975 government ordinance that stated that cheetahs were now a protected species and could be removed only in 'the interest of protection of one's life or property'. But for every female cheetah he traps, a farmer may catch upwards of ten males, because they are attracted to the trees used as scent posts where traps are often set. A farmer who finds that he cannot sell a cheetah he has caught is likely to shoot it. Returning

the few cheetahs who have been bred in captivity to the wild has rarely been successful, so it is imperative to protect the wild population by persuading farmers to help conserve cheetahs.

It was with this as a background that Laurie Marker and Lise Hanssen set to work to try to win over the ranchers. They realized that the future of Namibian wildlife lay in the hands of some thousand men. Only if they won their support was there any hope of a long-term future for the cheetah. It quickly became apparent that, as is so often the case in the war between farmers and predators, the extent of the livestock losses had been exaggerated; the predator had become larger than life. Only in 3 per cent of cases was there actual evidence of cheetahs killing livestock. And far from eradicating the problem, shooting cheetahs had little impact on losses – there is always a reservoir of dispersing young adults looking to fill a vacuum, so when one cheetah died others simply moved into the void.

Laurie Marker founded CCF in 1990 with her then husband, Daniel Kraus. For 15 years before that she had specialized in the captive breeding of cheetahs in the United States. I had seen pictures of her at various fund-raising events across the US, adding glamour and excitement by appearing with a tame cheetah. When Laurie first realized the extent of the problem facing cheetahs in Namibia in the 1980s, she believed that the best solution was to catch them and place them in parks or zoos. But time was running out. The captive-breeding programme was never going to be sufficient to save the cheetah in the long term. Someone had to make a stand on the cheetah's behalf, so Laurie eventually packed up her belongings and moved to Otjiwarongo in Namibia.

On the other side of Otjiwarongo, Wayne and Lise Hanssen had initiated their own homegrown cheetah and leopard conservation organization, AfriCat, on the family ranch, Okonjima. Wayne had been

born and brought up on the ranch, and knew all about the difficulties cheetahs can pose for farmers: his father used to lose more than 20 calves a year to predators, and his response had been to reach for his gun. But Wayne and Lise wanted to try a different approach. By using guard animals and better fences and confining calves to pens at night, they managed to reduce losses and in the process persuaded Wayne's father to stop killing predators.

Neither AfriCat nor CCF ever says don't kill cats – they know that to do so would find little resonance with ranchers and they would run the risk of being dismissed as 'bunny huggers'. Certainly cheetahs do sometimes take livestock, and small animals such as lambs and kids also fall prey to caracals, jackals and baboons. Some years ago in the Mara we filmed a cheetah chasing a goat and saw for ourselves how easy it was for a fleet-footed predator to catch an animal that had lost much of its ability to evade predators – no deadly weapons to defend itself with, no blinding speed or alertness to deflect an attack. But it was also evident that when livestock is well guarded – as is generally the case in Masailand – it is almost impossible for a diurnal predator such as a cheetah to kill it. In this instance the Masai herdsmen came rushing in and chased the cheetah away, leaving the goat shocked but otherwise unharmed. Similarly, if sufficient wild prey is available, cheetahs tend to ignore livestock, which accounts for only 2 per cent of the prey they take, although on farms it makes up 65 per cent of available food. It is generally only when there is a decline in prey numbers and the livestock is to hand that they take to killing young calves – anything more than six months old is too big for them to kill easily – though old, sick or young cheetahs are easily tempted by the soft option offered by livestock, particularly if it is allowed to roam unattended.

Laurie and Lise realized that there was a lot that ranchers and smallholders could do

Laurie Marker has pioneered another novel method of predator deterrent by encouraging farmers to keep guard dogs to protect their herds – particularly small stock such as sheep and goats – capitalizing on the natural fear that all cats have of dogs. Man has an ancient relationship with guarding dogs, and none more so than the livestock owners in the rugged hill pastures of Turkey, who traditionally favour a 6,000-year-old breed known as the Anatolian Shepherd to help fend off wolves and bears. The Anatolian, a big, strong, intelligent dog with the look of a rangy Labrador, is ideal for keeping cheetahs at a distance. It is gentle yet protective, adapted to the heat of the day and the chill of cold nights, which equips it well for the harsh climate of the Namibian countryside. Unlike traditional sheep dogs, which earn their keep by herding the flock, Anatolians walk with the herd, providing a focus of attention for them, which is vital if they are to ward off a predator such as a cheetah which chases only running prey. When alarmed they have a deep bark, which both intimidates a predator and alerts the herdsman to danger.

There are now over 160 Anatolian shepherd dogs working on Namibian farms, with 75 per cent of farmers reporting a large decline in livestock losses.

Laurie Marker and the CCF have pioneered the use of Anatolian Shepherds to guard livestock against attacks by predators.

to reduce livestock losses; the Hanssens had proved this on their own ranch. When a rancher says, 'But predators are killing my livestock and endangering my livelihood', the first step is to find out what he is doing to lessen the temptation or likelihood that a predator will be able to do this. The time has come for livestock owners and game managers to help bear the cost and co-operate in predator management – which doesn't have to end up as a euphemism for killing – but many either can't be bothered or say it is too costly.

In Masailand a number of boys and young men guard the herds from the moment they leave the protection of the cattle boma shortly after first light until they return again at dusk. At night the cattle are herded inside the thornbush stockade surrounding the homestead, and young calves, goats and sheep are penned into a separate enclosure or even into one of the Masai's dung-covered houses. This keeps all but the most determined lion or leopard at bay, and by this time any cheetahs have probably hunkered down among a patch of long grass for the night. Cattle in Namibia have a distinct calving

season, but they are often allowed to give birth out in the open, making it easy for a predator to attack them. Now farmers are being persuaded to keep vulnerable calves close to the homestead or, better still, in a separate, well-protected enclosure for the first six to eight weeks, helping greatly to reduce losses.

Two of the oldest and least expensive methods of deterring predators are the use of donkeys and the keeping of more aggressive breeds of cattle that are better able to look after themselves. Donkeys can be very belligerent when threatened and, just like a zebra stallion, will fiercely resist attempts by predators to kill young animals. A donkey is just too big and powerful for a cheetah to grapple with and, knowing it can't outrun the cat, it will turn and hold its ground, biting and kicking fiercely. One farmer managed to reduce his losses almost to nil by integrating three female donkeys into his calving herd. And farms that maintained reasonable populations of wild prey suffered less predation of their livestock.

A female Anatolian called Boots, born in the USA in 1989 and imported into

Namibia in 1994, was the founder of CCF's Guarding Dog Programme. Anatolians guard whatever species they grow up with, which accounted for the fact that early one morning I found Boots and her companion Koya lying quite happily in Chewbaaka the cheetah's enclosure. Now eight years old, Chewbaaka was orphaned at the age of just three weeks and raised at CCF by Laurie. Having been denied the chance to refine his innate hunting abilities by associating with his mother, Chewbaaka can never be released back into the wild. Instead he has become the charismatic totem of CCF, fussed over by schoolchildren and presidents alike. Boots and Koya have known Chewbaaka since he arrived at CCF and 'guard' him just as they would a herd of goats or sheep.

Another and far more controversial way of conserving cheetahs and lessening the antipathy of ranchers towards them is to let wealthy trophy hunters shoot a limited number each year on the ranches. Trophy hunting has long been an important source of foreign exchange for Namibia, worth around US$1 million annually. Of the US$1,000 trophy fee paid to shoot a

Kudu near Chief's Camp, Okavango Delta, Botswana. Kudu calves are an important prey for cheetahs in Namibia.

cheetah, 15 per cent goes to a conservation fund, with the rest split between the guide and the farmer – often the same person. In theory, if a farmer can make money from hunting one or two cheetahs a year, he might tolerate all the others that move through his land. The challenge is in establishing realistic quotas and then persuading people to abide by them. In 1992, CITES approved a limited trade in Namibian, Zimbabwean and Botswanan cheetahs, setting an annual quota for Namibia of 150 for trophy hunting and export to approved zoological facilities in an attempt to reduce indiscriminate killing.

In many ways the story of the Namibian cheetah is a parable for our times, with wildlife and the environment struggling to find harmony under the influence of man. Some 120 years ago, before the first Europeans settlers arrived to colonize this desert wilderness, the herds of antelope and other prey animals moved seasonally according to the rains and the renewal of vegetation – and so did the predators. This helped to preserve the fragile balance between the wild animals and their

environment. Whenever the waterholes dried up and the grazing vanished, the herds moved on and the cheetahs followed. But once man started to fence off the land and create permanent sources of water by sinking boreholes for his livestock, the

cattle, the wild herds and the cheetahs were able to linger year round. As farms were fenced off, it became easier to remove wildlife, which was seen as direct competition to livestock, and the numbers of species such as kudu, gemsbok and

Zebras at dusk, Mombo Camp, Okavango Delta. In many parts of southern Africa game ranching has replaced cattle farming as a more economic use of the land.

springbok were reduced. Farmers also quickly killed off the more dangerous predators – by the 1950s lions and hyenas had been eliminated from the majority of the farmland. Removing these two top predators made it easier for the cheetahs and leopards to survive.

By the 1960s the loss of the wild migratory herds and severe overgrazing by livestock had caused a noticeable change in the vegetation. What had been primarily open savanna had begun to revert to bush, eventually leading to a massive reduction in cattle numbers on commercial farmlands between 1960 and 1990. In an effort to help the farmers, the government created economic incentives in 1967 by ceding ownership of huntable game on farms (excluding protected and specially protected species) to the landowners to encourage them to conserve wildlife by

utilizing it, in the hope that it would also help to create a better balance between livestock, wildlife and the environment. In the 1970s, the numbers of kudu, gemsbok and springbok increased dramatically, as did the cheetah population. But due to the migratory nature of much of Namibia's wildlife, 'ownership' was constantly changing, making it hard to estimate the real numbers of wild animals on each ranch. Some unscrupulous landowners took advantage of the situation, over-utilizing what was in reality a communal resource, even to the extent of opening their fences during times of migrations, then closing them again and trapping the animals on their land to maximize the amount of money they could make from hunting, game cropping for meat, hides and curios, and selling surplus animals to other ranches or game reserves. In addition to this, during

the 1970s the country experienced one of its periodic wet cycles, promoting good grass growth that caused farmers to overstock by a magnitude of two or three times the recommended number of cattle.

By the end of the decade the worst drought in a hundred years was beginning to take its toll on all those cattle and, even though farmers desperately tried to stem the tide by destocking, the process of land degradation was already underway. The grasslands vanished beneath a tide of thickets and much of it reverted to heavy bush. This prompted many of the farmers to catch and sell the wild animals on their land as a way of protecting the pastures for their domestic animals – and of raising money to see them through the lean times. Some set aside all or part of their land for game ranching and trophy hunting, particularly in the north, where wildlife was

Honey's four-month-old cubs climbing down from a boscia tree they had scrambled up when a hyena approached.

still abundant. The outcome of all these changes was that between 1983 and 1986 the three major game species – kudu, gemsbok and springbok – declined by 60 per cent. Many of the game ranches did not have electric fences to deter predators, and exotic game species such as black-faced impala and blesbok, imported from South Africa, were not necessarily used to avoiding cheetahs and leopards and proved easy prey. Because wildlife on game ranches now had a price on its head, any losses to predators were viewed as an economic disaster, encouraging landowners to shoot or trap the big cats.

During the rainy years the cheetah population had flourished, but when the drought took hold again and wildlife numbers declined so dramatically they faced a new problem. Between 1977 and 1986 the kudus were hit by a severe rabies epidemic. Kudu calves are one of the cheetah's main prey and a decline in other suitable prey during this same period meant that it was even more tempting for the cats to turn their attention to livestock. The ranchers responded by intensifying their war against the cheetah. According to CITES, between 1980 and 1991 6,818 cheetahs were removed from the Namibian population (5,670 killed in protection of livestock, 958 exported and 190 killed by trophy hunters), with the number of deaths peaking at nearly 900 in 1982. Though this is undoubtedly an underestimate – not all removals are reported – it resulted in a 50 per cent decline in the cheetah population. The situation had reached an all-time low, with farmers maintaining that cheetahs were the most serious wild animal threat to their livestock and blaming them for large financial losses. The sight of cheetah spore was enough for some farmers to attribute the death of any calves to them, even though natural causes such as disease, poor nutrition and stillbirths were likely to be the real culprits. To exacerbate the situation, prior to independence many European farmers – fearing that their livelihood

Chewbaaka, CCF's charismatic cheetah, who was orphaned at the age of three weeks. Male cheetahs use certain easy-to-climb species of tree – known in Namibia as 'play trees' – as scent posts, depositing their faeces on the limbs and spraying scent against the trunk.

might be adversely affected – cashed in on their wildlife populations by selling game meat and by trophy hunting, further reducing the cheetah's prey base.

In 1984 Dieter Morsbach of the Department of Nature Conservation began his three-year study of the cheetah/rancher issue, which has since been followed up and expanded on by CCF. Morsbach had already helped to identify a number of significant differences in the behaviour of Namibian cheetahs. Both males and females were found in higher densities than their East African cousins, yet both ranged further: males had home ranges of up to 800km² (300sq. miles) and females up to 1,200km² (over 450sq. miles), with extensive overlap. Laurie Marker's more recent figures suggest that both males and females sometimes cover ranges up to twice this size, but make intensive use of a smaller core area. The size of the range is

Young male cheetah caught in a rancher's trap. Traps are often located at the base of 'play trees' or along fence lines.

generally inversely related to rainfall – in places with higher rainfall, prey is likely to be more abundant and the need to roam widely is lessened.

While trees are important scent posts for cheetahs in the Mara–Serengeti, in Namibia certain species are particularly significant: the camel thorn (*Acacia erioloba*), bastard umbrella-thorn acacia (*Acacia luederitzii*), weeping wattle (*Peltophorum africanum*) and shepherd's tree (*Boscia albitrunca*) have been identified. These 'play trees' or 'newspaper trees', as the ranchers call them, have been talked about for 30 years. The sloping trunk of the camel thorn is a particular favourite, as it is easy to climb and the large horizontal limbs are ideal for scanning the surrounding countryside. Cheetahs gravitate to these trees, spraying the trunk with their distinctive scent and leaving their droppings on the limbs.

Angie and I visited one such tree with Laurie and Chewbaaka. Chewbaaka had a regal bearing, and like thousands of people before us we indulged the chance to stroke his coarse fur, to hear him purr in contentment and to be tolerated by such an extraordinary creature. It was late afternoon, the time when the stark Namibian landscape is at its most beguiling, illuminated by soft light that turned the browns and ochres to delicate pastel shades. Chewbaaka headed straight for the distinctive silhouette of the giant camel thorn, pausing briefly to spray scent at its base before bounding effortlessly up the rutted trunk, sniffing for signs left by the wild cheetahs who regularly pass through the area and depositing a pile of his own smelly droppings to let the next cheetah know that he had been here first. All the adult cheetahs at CCF have a tree in their enclosure and every morning and evening they climb up it, sniffing for scent (reassuringly always finding their own), raking their claws to leave their scent and sharpen their claws, and then squatting to produce a pile of droppings in a prominent position on the limb.

Farms that do not have suitable play trees are known as 'pass through' farms, because cheetahs move quickly through on their way to the next tree. Farmers who are troubled by stock-killing cheetahs – and some who aren't – set traps at the base of these trees, surrounding both trap and tree with thornbush, making it impossible for a cheetah to reach the tree without entering the trap. These 2m (6ft 6in) long wire cages have drop doors at either end and a metal plate in the middle that acts as a trigger, causing the doors to close the moment an animal puts its weight on the plate. If a family of cheetahs or a coalition of males is involved, then the first cheetah caught is kept in a holding cage within the boma, and additional traps are set. The imprisoned animal's yips of distress attract its companions and they in turn are caught. When Laurie first started working with the farmers it quickly became obvious that many of them did not make any distinction between stock-killers and non-offenders. Any cheetahs who were caught were either killed or sold to zoos.

In 1992 CCF began ear-tagging cheetahs caught on farms and releasing them again to find out their movements, while other cheetahs were radio-collared and released at a research site surrounding the Waterberg Plateau. Within a year there were nine ear-tagged cheetahs and two with radio collars. Blood and tissue samples are taken from all captured cheetahs on the basis that the more information CCF can provide to farmers about the cheetahs the easier it will be to manage them effectively. So far over 250 farms covering 22,000km² (8,500sq. miles) have been surveyed by CCF in an effort to discover how many cheetahs – and what other species of animals, both livestock and wild prey – are living there. CCF also wanted to examine such things as management practices and attitudes to predators. Laurie reckons that the farmers fall into three categories – 50 per cent aren't too concerned about the cheetahs on their land and don't pose a

problem, 20 per cent are really positive in their attitude and 30 per cent are hard core, wanting nothing to do with conserving them. What is without question is that while livestock farmers can be persuaded to live with cheetahs, game farmers cannot, and what is needed is a mixed land-use management scheme.

Nowadays many of the farmers call CCF or AfriCat to collect any cheetahs they might catch, rather than killing them. Initially they were paid an incentive of US$250 per cheetah, but both organizations now oppose payment, as it might encourage people to set traps simply to make money. (The number of cheetahs removed from farms has dropped from an average of 19 in 1993 to two in 2002, highlighting the increased tolerance of the farmers, who are now more likely to target only those cheetahs who actually take livestock.) After a six-week quarantine period, healthy animals with no history of taking livestock are released in a private game reserve or farm in the same or a similar area. Livestock killers are relocated to a private, fenced reserve and/or fitted with a radio collar so that they can be monitored to see if they kill again. The only animals who are kept permanently are those who are old, sick or too young to be re-released.

In the past relocation of cheetahs in Namibia has not prospered. The first attempts were made in Etosha in the late 1960s, with further releases in the 1970s. Cheetahs who were subsequently monitored highlighted the difficulties they faced and were not successful, no doubt because the cats tried to return to their original home ranges and were shot as they moved south through farmland. Unmonitored and indiscriminate relocations are discouraged, as they often exacerbate problems for farmers, with the cheetahs targeting livestock when they are in unfamiliar territory or travelling from farm to farm in their attempt to reach home. However, relocations are now an

important part of the management of the cheetah population and under the right circumstances can be successful, as Luke Hunter proved at Phinda Game Reserve in South Africa. As always they need to be monitored, not least to let the ranchers know what the cheetahs are up to.

Laurie Marker is tackling the challenge of how best to protect Namibia's cheetah population on three fronts. Like Lise Hanssen, she works directly with ranchers to encourage them to trap but not kill 'problem' cheetahs. Taking a broader perspective, educating the general public – both children and adults – is a priority, teaching them about cheetahs and their importance to Namibia and the world by arranging visits to CCF's impressive education centre, and via newsletters and literature, visiting schools and working with the government. Laurie also supports efforts to boost the genetic variation among captive cheetahs by providing new blood from wild animals, but without compromising the wild population.

Because it is almost impossible to release a cheetah who has never learned to hunt back into the wild, there is always going to be a surplus of animals at places like CCF and the AfriCat Foundation that provide a home for such animals. Recently, Namibia's President Sam Njuma, who is a great supporter of Laurie's work and Patron of CCF, gave ten cheetahs to the President of the United States to help the captive-breeding programme that Laurie used to oversee. This conveniently circumvented the fact that it is now illegal to export animals from Namibia, endangered or otherwise. A strong case could be argued for a dispensation that would allow some of Namibia's captive cheetah population to be exported to boost the international captive-breeding programme, but the fear is that it might open the door to unscrupulous traders. The cheetah continues to be a valuable commodity, both as a trophy and as a zoo animal, and with the recent ban on its export the price paid by visiting hunters has soared to 15,000 rand (US$2,300). While Angie and I were visiting CCF and AfriCat, a report appeared in the Windhoek *Observer* highlighting the kind of problem facing the wildlife authorities. A number of cheetahs had been illegally transported at night by plane from a Namibian ranch to the Free State in South Africa; the case was under investigation.

Another possible way forward, pioneered by Laurie and other like-minded conservationists, is the creation of wildlife conservancies – collectives of game farms where fences are removed to allow free movement of animals. Eco-tourism and selective hunting are encouraged as a way of making these areas pay, and predators are managed as part of the ecosystem instead of on a farm-by-farm basis.

We were lucky enough to be at CCF when a call came in from a rancher who had trapped three cheetahs and wanted to know if Laurie could drive out and collect them. The answer was yes. Laurie spent the next hour on the phone, scrutinizing her map of the adjacent ranches, looking for the right person to call. She needed a rancher who would be sympathetic to having three cheetahs released on his land. Eventually she found the person she was looking for and we set off.

On our way to the ranch we stopped to buy some food at a dusty outpost called Hochvelt, which seemed to emerge from nowhere like a lonely frontier town in the Wild West – a single row of buildings, a bar at one end, the provision store at the other. A huge man sat behind the bar, talking to his two customers, one as massively built as he was, with dusty red eyes and day-old stubble, the other younger, shorter, but just as red-eyed, washing away the dust with a glass of beer. We were in a hurry and I had simply wanted to use their toilet, so I refused the offer of a drink, but knew that the word had already been passed that CCF was in town. The younger man got straight to the point: 'Cheetahs are bad. If a cheetah gets in among the calves they don't just kill one, they kill

many, just like a leopard. If I see a cheetah on my place I blast it – simple as that. Ours is a hunting ranch, we have a hundred springbok, that's money, I don't want cheetahs getting into them.' Many of the ranchers have found that game is more valuable than cattle – a cow is worth US$300, a kudu trophy head US$900, and the rancher gets to keep the meat.

When I spoke to Laurie later she confirmed that cheetahs do sometimes make multiple kills when they find themselves among domestic stock, just like a fox in a chicken coop. It is only natural that a predator which normally has to work hard to take a single wild animal should kill without restraint given the opportunity. It is irrelevant to talk of blood lust or ruthless wanton killers. As George Schaller said when defending the poor reputation that wild dogs earned themselves for their manner of killing,

Nature has neither cruelty nor compassion. The ethics of man are irrelevant to the world of other animals. Dogs kill out of necessity, in innocence not in anger, hardly a situation to engender revulsion on the part of man…. Periods when prey can be easily caught are rare indeed in the life of a predator.

When we arrived at the Lindenhof Hunting Ranch, Hartmut the manager greeted us. Hartmut was also the ranch's professional hunter; lean and weather-beaten, he wore high lace-up boots, khaki trousers and a battered bush hat. Straight away it was evident that he was concerned about the cheetahs he had caught, that he was interested in Laurie's work and that he wanted to know more about cheetahs. Certainly he was not enamoured of cheetahs who killed stock or game animals destined to be trophies – they were his livelihood – but he was prepared to compromise.

Hartmut told us that the best place to set traps was along the fence, so as to catch the cheetahs as they were looking for a

place to escape or to get at play trees. He guided us to the spot where the three cheetahs had been trapped. He had picked up their tracks as he walked round the ranch, and had only acted when it became apparent that the cheetahs weren't just passing through – if they had been, he would have let them be. Three large metal traps were set in a single line along the fence and covered with branches to make them less conspicuous. Traps such as these are unselective in what they catch. Even oryx, which tend to crawl under fences rather than jump over them, have been known to find their way inside. Some animals injure themselves as they fight to break free, but fortunately cheetahs are not as volatile as leopards, who often end up with broken teeth or a battered face as they charge around. If the rancher checks his traps daily things are not so bad, but some leave them unattended for days at a time.

Warthogs are a particular menace to fencing, and with their rock-hard snouts can burrow under just about anything, creating holes that can become predator highways or an escape route for valuable game. One solution – rather than employing gin traps that are cruel and indiscriminate – is to use electric fencing, with one strand 15cm (6in) off the ground and 15cm (6in) out from either side of the fence, with a second strand 30cm (12in) from the ground to shock predators when they try to cross. A third wire placed even higher will stop any predator that attempts to climb the fence without touching the lower wires. Warthogs can withstand intense pain if they are determined to break through a fence, but using electrified barbed wire for the bottom strand and a higher shock can stop them.

Hartmut carefully stripped the branches from the cages, trying not to agitate the cheetahs. He had placed a bowl of water in each cage. The cats – three young males aged about 14 to 18 months – stared out at us with baleful eyes, slapping the ground with their forepaws in an impressive threat

Kike had dragged this kill – an adult male Thomson's gazelle – into the cover and shade offered by my vehicle. But she still made sure to stay alert.

Male Thomson's gazelle watching a cheetah. All prey animals try to maintain a safe distance, called their 'flight distance', between themselves and predators.

The largest of the three weighed 32kg (70lb), which put him at the lower end of the normal adult weight range. They were almost certainly brothers who had recently left their mother, branching out on the road to independence. This is a difficult time for young cheetahs. They are still not competent hunters, though with three of them it was more likely that they might obtain a meal, even if they did have to share it. These three were fortunate that they had been caught by Hartmut; they

gesture, teeth bared, hissing or lunging against the sides of the cage in an attempt to escape as we approached. As quickly as we could we moved the cheetahs into the three wooden crates we had brought with us. Hartmut and his wife Gisella had kindly offered us overnight accommodation in the hunting lodge, so we transferred the cheetahs to an outhouse and anaesthetized them. Everyone was assigned a job: blood and tissue were taken for DNA work, a numbered ear tag was fitted and a tiny transponder inserted under the skin above the root of the tail so that the cheetah could always be recognized if recaptured, by scanning and reading the code. The cats were weighed and measured, everything from length of body and limbs to size of testes, all recorded on a detailed fact chart.

Laurie pointed out some of the features that indicate inbreeding in cheetahs: the kinked tail, the raw cavity worn in the upper palate by the tip of one of the lower molars, the crowded lower incisors. But in general the three cheetahs were in excellent physical condition; their coats had a

healthy sheen to them and there were no signs of wounds or parasites, bar the odd tick. Their teeth sparkled and, despite their ordeal in the traps, thanks to Hartmut's consideration in providing them with water they were well hydrated.

We rose early next morning to check on the cheetahs and feed them. Hartmut had given us a whole leg of beef for the purpose. Laurie handed me a piece of wire twisted into a hook at one end and baited with a chunk of meat. I pushed the wire through one of the gaps between the slats of the wooden crates. The cheetah spat as I lent forward, then, without taking his eyes off me, gingerly opened his mouth and reached towards the meat, pulling it off the end of the wire. Under similar circumstances a leopard would have gone ballistic, but cheetahs are very different. Over the next half-hour each cheetah took some 2kg (4½lb) of meat. They were hungry. On an empty stomach a cheetah can consume a quarter of its body weight, and will do so given the chance, operating on a feast-or-famine regime like all predators.

would at least be given a second chance of fending for themselves in the wild. Another rancher might have ended it right there by shooting all three of them. But as Hartmut had said to Laurie, 'Let's see what happens. If they come back, we will have to talk again.' By this he meant that next time he would want a reassurance from Laurie that the cheetahs had either been moved far away from the ranch or found a new home in captivity. You couldn't ask for better than that (around 180 cheetahs are still known to be killed by farmers each year, though nobody can be sure if all the animals killed are reported).

As we said goodbye to Hartmut and Gisella, they turned to Laurie and said, 'Thank you for looking after our cheetahs.' It was spoken sincerely, not gratuitously; they needed to make a living, but also wanted to see wild land survive – and the cheetahs too. We drove for half an hour down the road until we reached the ranch belonging to the farmer who had agreed to the cheetahs being set free on his land. Then we released them back into the wild. Knowing how hard it is for a cheetah mother to raise any of her cubs to independence, I could only wish these youngsters well as they raced away. They certainly couldn't ask for better friends than Laurie and Hartmut. By working together they are giving the Namibian cheetah its best chance of survival.

Kike and three nine-month-old cubs feeding on a gazelle fawn at dusk. A cheetah mother normally allows her cubs to feed first, often ending up with just the scraps from a small kill.

The Last Place on Earth

Namibia had been an eye-opener for Angie and me: a beguiling land full of contrasts and contradictions. It seemed ironic that this hauntingly beautiful country was indeed a vital stronghold for wild cheetahs, yet some of the people who lived on the land still considered them to be a nuisance at best. There was no middle ground when it came to competition – man was proving to be as ruthless in his persecution of cheetahs as the lion. In Namibia the cheetah is an elusive creature for visitors, almost as difficult to see as the Phantom, the shy male who so often eluded David and Lida Burney during their stay in the Mara Triangle. Now our thoughts turned back to our home in East Africa, to the flesh-and-blood creature that is the cheetah.

In January 2004, when Angie and I returned to the Mara to try to meet up with Kike and her cubs again, it was as if we had continued south into the Serengeti. A huge expanse of the Mara's rolling plains had been burned a few weeks earlier in the hope that rain was imminent, and sure enough when it did rain the land turned overnight into an oasis of green, drawing the plains game back into the reserve. It was awash with a sea of animals – wildebeest in their tens of thousands grazed alongside large herds of zebras and Thomson's gazelles. It reminded me of my first view of the Serengeti's short-grass plains early one rainy season, though right now most of the rest of the Mara appeared to be in the midst of a drought. We had tracked the dry conditions from the moment we left Nairobi, dropping down the steep wall of the Great Rift Valley that beckons to travellers as they journey west. Wooden stalls perched at the edge of the rock face sell trinkets to visitors who stop long enough to capture the dramatic scenery with their cameras. Sheepskin rugs and shiny metal wheel rims that have fallen off vehicles compete with wildlife paintings, batiks, Masai spears and beadwork. But business is slow.

These have been depressing times for the hawkers, and they beckon to passing vehicles more in desperation than anything else, hoping at least to earn a few shillings by selling roasted maize cobs to passing truck drivers. Tourism is in trouble, and Kenya's craftsmen and tour operators are still suffering the repercussions of travel advisories issued by Britain and the United States in May 2003 and the fall-out from negative press reports based on the threat of terrorism and a general perception of insecurity fuelled by the international press. Most Kenyans are filled with despair by this, in the same way that they were outraged when terrorists bombed the American Embassy in Nairobi in 1998, killing 200 people and injuring 5,000 innocent Kenyans. The American government still refuses to rescind the travel advisory warning their nationals against travelling to Kenya. Yet where is safe from terrorism? Surely by not travelling people are playing into the hands of the terrorists – and missing the holiday of a lifetime, at the cost to Kenya's economy of nearly US$40 million.

Thankfully the wildebeest know nothing of travel restrictions and continue to migrate around the Mara–Serengeti with complete freedom. They acknowledge no passports or border crossings, no fences to impede their right of passage, which dates back at least a million years. Yet, changeless though it may seem, there is nothing predictable about the timing of the migration. It all depends on the rains, and these days who knows when the rain will start and when it will end?

As filming of *Big Cat Week* drew to a close in October 2003, the afternoon skies had begun to fill with clouds and I thought that perhaps on this occasion the rains would begin on time, at least by the standards of earlier years, when you could depend on the first showers speckling the plains in mid-October. But it was not to be. November came and went, and then December, with nothing more than a few scattered showers. By then the last of the long grass had been eaten back and everywhere you looked the ground was dry and brown. Hippos wandered about during the daytime, desperately searching for

Masai women welcoming visitors to the Mara. They share their land with the Marsh Pride, Zawadi and Kike, who live part of their lives outside the reserve among the Masai herdsmen.

Zebras and wildebeest are constantly alert to the danger posed by lions staking out water-holes and river-crossing sites in the hope of ambushing prey.

sufficient to eat, their broad telltale pathways snaking for kilometres out into the plains, leading them far from the sanctuary of the river. But all that remained for them was the chewed stubble of rank grass. As the sun beat down, the hippos' dark hides oozed beads of red oily sweat in an attempt to keep the massive animals from dehydrating and to protect their sensitive skins. The buffaloes, another water-dependent species, were also showing signs of distress as they wandered listlessly from one dried-out wallow to another, their pelvic bones jutting from beneath their ragged skins, making them a target for the lions. But drought and deluge mould savanna Africa, keeping the animals in harmony with their environment.

Once more the wildebeest dominated the landscape, just as they always do when the migration is present. But where were these animals coming from, we wondered? If the rains had started in mid-October, the Serengeti herds would already have travelled the 200km (125 miles) back to the southern plains, reaching their destination

by early December. With the failure of the rains, perhaps the herds had been forced to delay their march, tarrying longer than usual in the Mara and around Seronera in the centre of the Serengeti, areas which receive more rain than the short-grass plains and support longer grasses. Alternatively – and more likely – many of the wildebeest now feasting in the Mara were part of the resident population that traditionally spends the rainy seasons on the Loita Plains to the east of the reserve, where they calve, moving back into the Mara only during the dry season, when they mingle with the Serengeti herds.

Wherever they might have come from, we couldn't believe the number of animals that now crowded onto the Mara plains. As the wildebeest rotated around the leafy, protein-rich pastures, they scattered the land with piles of fresh droppings, fertilizing the soil – and even as they cut back the grass their saliva was working its miracle, helping to promote cell division in the plants, fuelling the cycle of regrowth.

We drove down to the river-crossing sites on Paradise Plain, on the off chance that Kike and her cubs had moved west again. These were frustrating times. Kike always

seemed to keep one step ahead of our efforts to locate her, such a contrast to the intensity with which we had watched her and the cubs during the filming of *Big Cat Week*. At one point she had moved even further east than where we had last seen her, trekking onwards past the Talek Gate, trying to keep pace with the appetites of her three cubs, who by now were as large as she was. We kept expecting to hear that she had abandoned her offspring and wondered if she might already be pregnant with her next litter.

We could find no sign of Kike and the cubs on Paradise Plain, but just as Angie was preparing to head back to our home in Nairobi to start editing the slides for this book, we received a message telling us about another cheetah with four young cubs who were being seen regularly on the other side of the river in the Mara Triangle. It was now early April and though I was still keen to catch up with Kike again, we wanted to get some photographs of a cheetah with small cubs, so I decided to stay on for another two weeks to capitalize on the situation – and hopefully have one final meeting with Kike and her cubs before they split up.

Wildebeest and young calves on the short-grass plains of the Serengeti during the rainy season – the time when the wildebeest give birth to their calves.

I packed my bags and headed for Little Governor's Camp on the other side of the river. The Triangle is familiar territory for Angie and me, though I knew that I was in for an eventful time, as this area receives more rain than anywhere else in the Mara. The plains here are dominated in places by stands of *Balanites aegyptica* – the desert date – that look rather like acacia trees, even to the extent of having thorns. The undersides of the trees are browsed in a neat line by giraffes, and young cheetahs love to try to clamber up the wrinkled bark.

The rains continued intermittently over the next few days, the air sultry to humid, darkening the sky with tall thunderheads that would finally burst open, sending the rain pelting down in the late afternoon and on into the night. Where before everywhere had been a carpet of short grass, now the land began to disappear beneath kilometre after kilometre of long red-oat grass. Just getting around without sinking into the black-cotton soil was a challenge, and cars were forced to create new tracks across the land simply to avoid getting bogged down. I had been told where to search for the mother cheetah by one of the pilots who at sunrise each morning launch hot-air balloons from Little Governor's Camp, floating over the river and onwards across the plains. Recently the pilots and drivers had seen the cheetah mother and her four-month-old cubs on an almost daily basis during their mid-morning game drives, and at times even spotted them from the balloon, tiny specks making their way through the lengthening grass. The cubs had been born in late November in a thicket near the border with the Serengeti. Since then the family had moved 25km (16 miles) to the north. At least now that the cubs were old enough to follow their mother – and they had been for the past two months – she could wander more extensively in search of prey.

Much of the game had disappeared from the low-lying marshy ground that characterizes the land close to the river, and

Honey with four five-month-old cubs in the Mara Triangle. There are fewer lions and hyenas here than in the rest of the Mara, a fact which indirectly helps the cheetah to flourish.

had moved to the higher, better-drained areas along the base of the escarpment where the grass was still relatively short. But there was a distinct lack of Thomson's gazelles and impalas in the area, certainly compared with the number you see when the wildebeest are in residence and the grass is cropped to within a couple of centimetres or so of the ground; then the plains are swarming with gazelles feasting

Honey and cubs. By this age – five months – the cubs are used to following their mother wherever she leads them in pursuit of food for them all.

on the regrowth and it is possible to see half a dozen cheetahs in a morning. I was anxious to see if this female was either Honey or the other cheetah that Simon and Warren had filmed in September 2002, both of whom had had three cubs at the time. A third female had given birth to five cubs just as we finished filming that series, so it might even be her. I would be able to tell by checking the photographs Angie had taken when she was acting as a spotter for the cheetah team.

Whoever the cheetah was, it was a remarkable achievement for her to have raised four offspring even to this age – one rarely sees this many cubs in the Mara once they have left the den. Even though cheetahs here do not seem to suffer such high cub mortality as they do in the Serengeti, it is still usually 50 per cent or more. And now, with the cubs growing rapidly, their mother might struggle to find sufficient food for them all. Only by continuing to move would she manage to do that.

Later that afternoon I followed the directions I had been given and found a number of vehicles gathered on an area of short grass at the foot of the escarpment. It was the cheetah mother. She was resting on a termite mound with her four cubs tucked close together in a pile around her legs – a picture of contentment. But to my horror I noticed that the whole family was suffering from some form of mange. The inside of the mother's ears were brown and crusted with scab, so too were the cubs' ears; one of them was particularly badly affected, with its elbows and the skin on its forehead and under its chin showing signs of damage. Now what were we going to do? I found myself racked with uncertainty – was it right for us to interfere? Surely, I reasoned, cheetahs are an endangered species and one of the animals that visitors most want to see on safari – and without the revenue from tourism, wildlife refuges like the Mara would not survive. There is no point in deceiving ourselves that the

Mara – or any other park or reserve – isn't 'managed' and altered by human presence. Much as I agree in principle that we should allow nature to run its course, there is no point in being too rigid in interpreting that ideal, so long as we aren't adversely affecting any of the other cheetahs in the process.

As the sun dropped below the clouds, bathing the plains in soft light, the cheetah mother stood up, stretched, yawned and then set off along the main road, the cubs trotting along behind her. She veered off into the long grass and suddenly the cubs found themselves buried among the long seed-heads, which even their mother found it difficult to see above, emerging every so often to climb onto a termite mound to navigate the way ahead. The female looked wary, hardly surprisingly with four small cubs to protect. A pride of lions would have no difficulty in running the cubs down in such thick vegetation, but fortunately there were not many lions in the area, and I hadn't seen a hyena in the past few days either. The cheetah mother was taking no chances, however, moving from mound to mound as she made her way across the plains; that was how she had managed to keep the cubs safe, by staying alert. But there was nothing for her to hunt here – nothing that I could see, at least. Was this part of the problem, I wondered? Was the stress of trying to feed four cubs too much for her, making her susceptible to an infection that she had then passed on to the cubs? Had the pressure of vehicles been a factor?

The following morning I was delighted to find the family huddled around a male Thomson's gazelle that the Triangle female, as we had named her, had just killed. She lay next to the carcass, panting heavily, cooling herself down while her cubs 'worried' the dead gazelle, repeatedly grabbing it by the throat and pulling it around. Then the family all settled down to feed. Within 30 minutes they had eaten the meat from the thighs, neck, ribs and along

Honey had caught a male Thomson's gazelle that soon attracted a large number of vultures. She was constantly sitting up to check for the approach of other predators. Fortunately she and her cubs had eaten a sizeable meal by the time the old Marsh lioness Khali trotted into view.

Honey's cubs reacted immediately to their mother's growl of warning and scattered. Honey confronted Khali, giving the cubs time to escape, but was then forced to move aside and allow the lioness to steal the remains of her kill.

Khali is very old and finding it difficult to secure enough food. She had left the rest of her pride and crossed the river to try her luck in the Triangle – and on this occasion was successful.

the spine. Their tummies were swollen, but now it was a race against the clock as vultures began to pour from the sky, alerting any lions or hyenas in the vicinity to the possibility that another predator had killed. And sure enough a predator had taken note. As the vultures edged closer, attempting to drive the cheetahs from their meal, the mother suddenly turned and then froze – just for a second – before arching her back and lowering her head, hackles raised, confronting the old lioness she saw running towards her. She moved forward another metre, growling with that characteristic whinnying moan that cheetahs use when faced with danger in the form of a larger predator. The cubs had already scattered, running for their lives, and once their mother was sure that they were safely on their way she turned and trotted after them.

I searched with my binoculars to try to identify the lioness. She was painfully thin and had a familiar pattern to her nose. It was Khali from the Marsh Pride. She must have temporarily abandoned her pride in her quest for food and crossed the river in the hope of better luck. She was in terrible condition, half-starved, running feebly up to the kill and grabbing it with her worn-down canines. Most of the flesh was gone, but it was meal enough.

Having checked on the position of the cheetah family, who by now had moved well away from the kill and were resting under a tree, I headed towards Serena Lodge, which is perched high up on a wooded hilltop offering spectacular views over the Mara River and Paradise Plain. From here you have an eagle's eye view of two of the traditional wildebeest river-crossing sites, where each year thousands of wildebeest, zebras and sometimes even Thomson's gazelles come down to drink and cross in their search for fresh grazing during the dry season, sending the massive crocodiles into a feeding frenzy. But now, with the long rains beginning in earnest,

Crocodiles feeding on a zebra they have just killed. Crocodiles grab hold of a large carcass and then use their powerful tails to spin and twist, tearing off chunks of meat.

Honey and cubs at the edge of the Mara River. The river itself is no impediment to the movement of cheetahs – or the other big cats – but they have to be wary of the crocodiles.

the area looked strangely empty; the first wildebeest wouldn't arrive until the beginning of the dry season in June. My reason for coming here now was to talk to Jonny Baxendale about the exciting developments that had been taking place in the Mara Triangle since 2001 – and, if I could, to find out more about the cheetah mother and see what could be done to help her.

Jonny Baxendale is the Senior Wildlife and Tourism Officer with the Mara Conservancy, a Not for Profit Company established in January 2001 to manage the Mara Triangle on behalf of the Trans Mara County Council, which holds the area in trust on behalf of the local community, primarily Masai pastoralists. When I first came to live in the Mara, both sides of the river were administered by the Narok County Council, but in 1995 the central government decided to create two districts where there had formerly been one. This meant that two different county councils suddenly administered the Mara.

Regardless of who is in charge, the Mara desperately needs to be cherished as one of the world's most important wildlife sanctuaries, an area that holds a priceless inventory of animal species and is a national asset worth millions of dollars to Kenya's tourist industry. Anything less is a disservice to the Masai people who have traditionally shown such a long-standing tolerance towards wildlife. So when the Trans Mara County Council signed a five-year management agreement with the Mara Conservancy it was a breath of fresh air, bringing hope that the downward trends could be reversed to the benefit of both wildlife and local people.

The Conservancy has provided a model for the management of similar wildlife areas in Kenya. The ranger force in the Mara Triangle is relatively small but highly efficient, with 35 rangers of whom 25 are operational at any one time. A further 12 rangers are currently undergoing training, and there is one senior warden and three wardens. Poaching has finally been brought

under control; during the last two and a half years, the anti-poaching team has confiscated nearly 2,000 snares and apprehended and prosecuted almost 300 individuals. Prior to this, gangs of Luo poachers from the Lake Victoria region plied their trade along the Mara River, taking hippos and anything else that got caught up in their snares, with little fear of being apprehended. But most of the poachers were Wakuria tribesmen from northern Tanzania and had to cross the Triangle, so the Conservancy's success in stemming this influx has helped greatly reduce poaching on the Narok side of the Mara, too.

The Wakuria are tough, cattle-herding people who live on both sides of the Kenya/Tanzania border, and Wakuria poachers were the bane of Myles Turner's life when he was Warden of the Serengeti from 1956 to 1972. I remember him showing me a photograph of the severed heads of 40 buffaloes taken in snares set in just one thicket. In recent years the

Honey's cubs showing signs of mange, often an indication that the animal is not in the best of health. Sadly the little male cub on the left of the picture did not survive – note how encrusted his left ear is.

Wakuria on the Kenya side of the border have tended to abandon their old hunting traditions and taken to farming, much to the relief of their neighbours the Masai, who used to bear the brunt of their cattle-rustling ways.

By combining forces with their counterparts in the field force in northern Serengeti for weekly patrols, the Mara Triangle rangers have kept the poachers on the back foot. This has resulted in increased security for the people living beyond the Mara Reserve boundary, with eight community scouts patrolling the area along the Siria Escarpment – the western boundary of the reserve – operating in pairs with their own radio frequency so that they can remain in communication with headquarters at all times. This has all but eliminated stock theft along the escarpment, which had been the bane of the villagers' lives for as long as I can remember. The scouts have the trust of the local community and get to know what is happening in the area, reporting to headquarters on the movement of strangers acting suspiciously. But perhaps

the most important gain for the local people has been the marked improvement in revenue collection.

For the first time, meaningful sums of money are being passed on to the landowners. The County Council, through the Mara Conservancy, reinvests 45 per cent of the revenue collected from visitors' daily entrance fees (US$30 for non-residents) and their vehicle fees (US$6) – 36 per cent to meet the cost of running the Mara Triangle and 9 per cent to pay the professional accounting firm Earth View, which collects the revenue. Virtually nothing is lost. Of the remaining 55 per cent, 36 per cent goes to the Trans Mara County Council and 19 per cent to the local community living in the group ranches bordering the Triangle. At last the local people with whom the future wellbeing of the Mara and its surrounds rests are beginning to see substantial sums – currently about US$143,000 per annum – paid to them through the Siria–Mara Trust, helping to ensure that the people who live alongside the reserve boundary see some financial incentive for continuing to tolerate wildlife on their private land. After all, as in

Namibia, predators sometimes wreak havoc with livestock, while the burgeoning elephant population can be a menace to life and livelihood, particularly when they leave the reserve and raid farmers' crops just when they are ready for harvest.

For years people have complained that the Mara is overutilized – that there are too many camps and lodges in and around the reserve – and for that reason various moratoriums have been tried to prevent yet more development. With a total of 48 facilities in the Greater Mara (the reserve and its immediate surrounds), there are 2,250 beds available, as well as numerous public campsites. Based on 30 per cent occupancy year round, this would represent approximately US$7 million; calculated at 50 per cent occupancy the figure rises to US$12 million, surely more than enough to implement major improvements. Kenya is enjoying a new government for the first time in nearly 30 years and a refreshing sense of optimism seems to be sweeping the country, bringing the hope that every part of the Mara will soon see better times.

Going hand in hand with an oversupply of accommodation is the question of off-road driving and animal harassment. The Mara Conservancy takes a pragmatic view of this. Instead of trying to enforce a ban on all off-road driving, they simply ask that drivers keep to the tracks until they sight a predator (or something equally significant such as elephants or rhinos). Then, and only then, may they leave the track in order to approach their quarry, and they are requested to return to the track they were originally on, rather than establishing a new pathway. Quite apart from making a major effort to keep the main road arteries to and from the various camps, lodges and entrance gates in good working order – applying murram and grading them when and where necessary – the Conservancy has also used a gyro mower to mark out over 230km (144 miles) of additional tracks.

It is remarkable how much a small, dedicated group of people can achieve with a grader, a lorry, two pick-ups and Cheetah One – the short-wheel-base Suzuki purchased with money donated by the BBC Natural History Unit on behalf of *Big Cat Diary* to help monitor the cheetah population and encourage visitors and drivers to treat the cheetahs with respect. The ranger in Cheetah One can tune in to all the frequencies used by drivers. They are asked not to surround a cheetah, so as not to prevent it from searching for prey or avoiding danger, and to keep a minimum of 15–20m (50–70ft) away, unless the cheetah moves closer to the car of its own accord. Angie and I are now raising funds through Friends of Conservation for a similar initiative in partnership with the Narok Country Council.

Half the battle has always been to get the drivers and guides on your side, and many of them have been incredibly helpful to Angie and me, keeping us informed of interesting sightings and working with the entire *Big Cat Diary* team to enable us to capture the best possible footage. The fact that they earn substantial amounts of money in tips from clients at the end of a successful safari is a strong incentive for a minority to bend the rules in order to keep their visitors happy. For this reason the Conservancy now requires that all resident drivers and guides employed at the various camps and lodges pass their Kenya Professional Guides bronze exam (there are silver and gold awards, too). This means that drivers will at least have learned a minimum amount of information on being a guide, and must sign a code of conduct binding them to the reserve by-laws. The intention is eventually to require that *all* drivers possess this qualification – gone are the days (in the Triangle at least) when drivers were a law unto themselves and virtually immune from any kind of meaningful supervision. Now any person – driver, guide or visitor – who breaks the by-laws can be issued with a written warning from the official violation book carried by wardens and rangers, with a copy of the

Veterinary surgeon Dr Zahoor Kashmiri, Mara Conservancy rangers, staff from Olonana Camp and Ann Kent Taylor and her team of volunteers help to treat Honey and her cubs.

violation sent to the driver's company. This is a real wake-up call, because anyone who commits a further offence may be prohibited permanently from entering the reserve. And who would want that?

I told Jonny Baxendale about the cheetah mother and said that I was concerned to see the cubs showing such obvious signs of mange – it is not uncommon to see adults with wear and tear along the margins of their ears, but this was much worse than that. Jonny suggested we contact Dr Zahoor Kashmiri, who lives on the Kenya coast and gives his time as a veterinary officer free of charge to the Kenya Wildlife Service (KWS). In fact everyone helps: Governor's Camp and Serena Lodge donate accommodation and all the air charter companies who fly into the Mara are only too willing to provide Dr Kashmiri with free flights. By chance he was coming to the Mara the following day to treat a three-month-old bull elephant calf who had been attacked and badly wounded during the night by lions – his tail had been almost cut in two, and he was suffering from multiple bites and a horrific wound to his bottom; in the end he had to be put down.

After consultation with the senior veterinary officer at KWS, Dr Kashmiri recommended that the cheetah mother and her four cubs be immobilized before their condition deteriorated any further, as the likelihood of their recovering without treatment was slim. I had watched the cubs carefully during the past week and the young male who was most seriously affected seemed to be weaker than his brothers and sister. He was slower to join in the frantic games of chase and tag in which fit and well-fed cubs of this age constantly indulge, and he was noticeably less robust when he did get caught up in the rough and tumble – and a step or so slower when the time came to move on with their mother.

Using syringes loaded with an immobilizing drug, Dr Kashmiri expertly darted the Triangle female and her cubs. As soon as they were sufficiently sedated, the team of volunteers that had quickly assembled set to work, moving the five cheetahs on to a tarpaulin. (The cubs were later placed in individual open-topped boxes to recover.) My first thought was how much bigger they looked than I had

Honey's cubs seemed determined not to lose sight of their mother once they were reunited after being treated for mange. The bird-like yip used by mother cheetahs to call and relocate their cubs is vital to their safety – cubs respond with an even higher pitched 'chirp' of their own.

When Angie and I last saw Kike – in the Rhino Ridge area in April 2004 – her cubs were as large as she was and almost ready to strike out on their own. By now we hope that Kike is pregnant again.

imagined. We took it in turns to wet their spotted fur to prevent them from overheating, making sure that they remained on their sides with their necks extended so as not to interfere with their breathing, and covering their eyes. Now that we could take a proper look at them, we could see the damage that the mange had caused to their skin, let alone their general health. It was even worse than we had thought, particularly in the case of the badly affected cub. Dr Kashmiri washed their ears and removed the scabs down to the bare flesh, then treated them with a herbal mixture called Multicare that he has found works wonders as an antibacterial and repels the biting flies that can cause bleeding and secondary infections. Each cheetah was then given an injection to treat

the mange, as well as a long-lasting antibiotic. Dr Kashmiri felt that this should suffice, but if the immature forms of the parasite did not succumb to this first dose, the treatment could be repeated in two weeks' time.

The most nerve-wracking moment came when it was time for the cheetahs to wake up and they were given a reversing agent to bring them round. The four cubs were on their feet and out of their boxes within a few minutes, chirping frantically for their mother. She remained woozy for a while longer and when she did get up it was obvious that she wanted nothing to do with the cubs – in fact she seemed alarmed by them and headed off in the opposite direction, refusing to call them. We all sat there, feeling sick with anxiety now that the

elation of having been able to treat the whole family had worn off. I began to have serious regrets about our decision to intervene.

At this age cheetah cubs rarely let their mother out of their sight, except when she is hunting and suddenly disappears over the horizon. The problem now was that they would not move towards her – even though they could see her standing 20m (70ft) away – until she called them, letting them know that it was safe to approach. This is a vital part of the way mother and cubs communicate, helping to prevent youngsters from wandering about when their mother is not there to look out for them, and making sure that they check first that it really is 'mother' and not some other cheetah or a leopard.

Eventually the female put us out of our misery; after wandering off to the river to drink – a distance of about 1km (⅔ mile) – she retraced her steps. We had remained with the cubs in case she did not return, preparing ourselves mentally for an uncomfortably chilly night in the car to try to ensure that the cubs came to no harm. Dr Kashmiri and I were just contemplating our options when the cubs suddenly got up and ran in the direction in which their mother had headed. Thank God, we thought, at least they were going the right way. We could see a herd of topis standing bolt upright facing the rise – it must be the mother cheetah.

Sure enough, it was. This time the cubs were taking no chances – and this time their mother was calling to them. They trotted towards her, stopping then starting again, unsure of themselves until she called a second time. As the first cub reached its mother it sniffed at her nose. She still seemed somewhat confused, almost as if she had temporarily forgotten that she had cubs and that these four anxious young cats milling around her legs were hers. But the cubs had no such doubts and as their mother moved away they followed, determined not to lose sight of her again.

I went to look for the cheetah family the following morning and after a long search found them huddled in the long grass around the base of a termite mound near where we had left them the previous evening. They all seemed fine, but sadly a day later one of the cubs was reported to be missing. By now Angie had returned from Nairobi and I had recrossed the river to search for Kike, but on hearing this news we hurried back to the Triangle. Ann Kent Taylor, a long-time Kenya resident who has done much to support anti-poaching in the Mara Triangle with her team of local volunteers and who had helped us treat the cheetahs, told us that when the family had last been seen together they were close to lions and a herd of buffaloes. Had there been an incident involving them, we

wondered? But when we caught up with them it became apparent that the missing cub was the little male who had been most seriously affected by the mange. Perhaps he had just been too weak to survive the stress of being immobilized.

Whatever the reason, we were devastated to have lost one of these unique creatures, whose mother had worked so hard to try to ensure their safety. But it is a harsh world that the cheetah inhabits, and surviving among so many predators is difficult enough. Our only consolation was that the Triangle female would probably have a better chance of raising her three surviving cubs – it would certainly be less stressful for her trying to find enough food. The good news was that Angie knew who this female was the minute she set eyes on her. It was Honey.

On our last day in the Mara before completing this book, Kike and her cubs reappeared. We could hardly believe our good fortune when Samuell Langat, who has worked in the Mara for 30 years and is one of our oldest friends among the drivers at Governor's Camp, waved us down to tell us the news. It had been four months since Kike had moved to the Intrepids area and apart from one brief visit to Rhino Ridge she seemed to have abandoned her old haunts. As the grass grew longer, she had no doubt decided to concentrate on places where prey was most abundant.

The following morning we were up before dawn, determined to make the most of these precious few hours before setting off for Nairobi. But search as we might we could find no trace of Kike and the cubs. Knowing how often they stayed huddled together hidden from view on a chilly morning, we circled back again, checking many of the places where we had seen her during the filming of *Big Cat Week*. Just as we were beginning to think that Kike had given us the slip yet again, Angie spotted a cluster of vehicles close to the place where she had told me she expected to find the cheetahs, on a gentle rise below the ridge.

How handsome and grown-up the three cubs now looked. For one glorious moment the family all perched on top of a termite mound, as if posing for a final portrait together. Then Kike spotted a gazelle and ran off in pursuit. As she closed in, the cubs raced alongside, running relays as they harried and cornered the

Kike and I at dusk. You would never allow a lion or leopard to do this.

bewildered prey. One of them reached out and slapped the gazelle's legs from underneath it, bowling it over and disappearing with it into the long grass. But before they had time to kill it, four young Marsh lions – desperate for food – came charging towards them, forcing the cubs to abandon their prey, which then quickly outpaced the slow-footed lions, escaping with its life.

Kike called to her cubs and they yipped in response, hurrying to join her as she led them away, heading back towards the Talek River once again. We knew that when we next saw them, the three young cheetahs would have left their mother, and Angie and I could only hope that by the time we began filming the next series of *Big Cat Week* in September, Kike would have given birth to a new litter of cubs with which to enthral us.

Gazetteer of big cat safari destinations

Setting out on a safari to Africa is the high point of many people's lives. For some it will be a journey of just a few weeks; for others it may mean the beginning of a new life, as it was for me when I left London in 1974 and joined a group of other young people travelling overland through Africa.

Most people who come on safari have high expectations, built on visions of wildlife captured in books or on television programmes such as *Big Cat Diary*. But these images can be deceptive, often relying on months or even years of waiting for the right moment, capturing events that happen only rarely. Consequently, when people arrive in the Mara they often expect – rather than hope – to see a leopard lounging in a tree in Leopard Gorge, to experience the thrill of having a cheetah jump on the bonnet of their car, or to watch lions pulling down a buffalo. But there are no guarantees about what you see on safari – just the promise that the experience will change you forever.

The biggest lesson Angie and I learned on our safari through southern Africa in 2001 was to throw away our expectations and enjoy whatever came our way. We had chosen destinations that we hoped would give us the best chance of seeing big cats. Some were famous for leopards or cheetahs, others places where all the big cats were said to be on view. Not all of them lived up to their reputation, not because it was undeserved, but because what we had hoped to see had happened yesterday or last week.

Due to time considerations we visited Namibia, Botswana, Zimbabwe, Zambia and South Africa in one continuous safari in the space of six weeks. The changing seasons can have a huge influence on what you see or don't see, so make sure you are travelling at the right time of the year for each destination when you plan your itinerary. If a place is 'good' for big cats, that implies that there's plenty for them to eat – the antelopes, gazelles, zebras and buffaloes on which they depend. By comparison with these prey species, predators are in the minority, so in looking for them you are guaranteed to find plenty of other animals to feast your eyes on. A safari is so much more than finding big cats. Nevertheless we have chosen places where we have experienced the best big cat watching. Our list is by no means exhaustive. There are many other areas out there waiting to be explored. Though cheetahs are the focus of this book we have included all three big cats in this review. The Insight guide *African Safari* and the Lonely Planet guides to *Watching Wildlife in East Africa* and *Southern Africa* are a mine of information for safari travellers.

Recommended destinations

Masai Mara National Reserve, Kenya

(1,510 km²/583 sq. miles)

This is one of the best places to see all three big cats, particularly lions. The rainy seasons are mid-October through to December (short rains) and April to June (long rains). The grass is at its longest after the long rains, making it more difficult to find predators, though you are virtually guaranteed to see lions at any time of year. The migration of wildebeest and

zebras usually arrives in June or July, with most of the herds returning to the Serengeti by the end of October.

September through to the end of March is our favourite time in the Mara, as the long grass retreats under a wave of animals. The best time to witness the great herds crossing the Mara River is from August to October – so September is a good bet, but no two years are the same. Even when the wildebeest and zebras depart the Mara it is still a beautiful place to visit, and with the grass short (and green during the rains of October–November) it is easier to find predators. The drier the year the better the predator viewing; the grass and bush are eaten back and stripped bare, making it easier to get around and see what is on offer.

The Mara is a birder's paradise, with more than 500 species. For accommodation, try Governor's Camp, Mara Intrepids or Mara River Camp. The Mara Triangle to the west of the river is excellent for cheetahs, though they are found throughout the reserve, and Little Governor's Camp, Olonana and Serena Lodge are among the best places to stay in the Triangle. If you prefer a private tented camp, East African Wildlife Safaris and Abercrombie and Kent are among a number of safari outfitters offering this option in Kenya.

Samburu National Reserve, Kenya

(104 km²/40 sq. miles)

One of the smaller reserves, but what a gem, providing a taste of northern Kenya, with excellent bird life. Any safari to Kenya should include a visit to Samburu. The scenery makes a wonderful contrast to the lush, rolling plains of the Mara, with stark rocky outcrops, dry bush country with towering termite mounds, and the palm-fringed Ewaso Nyiro River. To the south of the river lies Buffalo Springs National Reserve, which is equally good.

The dry seasons are best in Samburu, with plenty of activity around the river and large herds of elephants emerging from the forests to drink and cross. There are Grevy's zebras, gerenuks and reticulated giraffes – dry-country species that you don't find in the Mara.

Samburu and Buffalo Springs are famous for their leopards, and some of the camps and lodges put out bait in the evenings to attract nocturnal visitors. But you are quite likely to see leopards here during the day. There are lions and cheetahs, too, and wild dogs are occasionally seen. Among the best places to stay are Larsens tented camp and Samburu Serena Lodge.

Serengeti National Park, Tanzania

(14,763 km²/5,700 sq. miles)

The Serengeti would be worth a visit even if it didn't have any wildlife. The fact that it does – in the kind of abundance found in few other places – makes this one of our top five wildlife destinations worldwide.

The sheer expanse of the Serengeti plains, particularly in the rainy season when the massed herds of wildebeest and zebras darken the grasslands, is a sight to behold, with lions, hyenas and cheetahs all in attendance. The wildebeest cows give birth to their calves between January and March, so February is a good time to visit. The wildebeest leave the plains and head for the woodlands and water at the beginning of the dry season towards the end of May, streaming in their thousands through the spectacular Moru Kopjes. The more marked the transition between wet and dry seasons, the more dramatic the exodus from the plains. This is when the wildebeest begin their rut, and it is well worth heading for the Seronera area in the centre of the park, which has always been one of Africa's top leopard haunts. They frequently lie up among tall stands of yellow-barked acacia trees along the Seronera Valley or slump contentedly along the broad beam of a sausage tree. Seronera is also a good place to look for lions and cheetahs.

The rugged northern woodlands around Lobo are another good place to visit when the great herds are passing through in the dry season (June–October). Among the best places to stay when the herds are massed on the southern plains are Ndutu Lodge, overlooking Lake Lagarja, and Kusini Camp; with Serengeti Sopa Lodge within easy reach of Moru, Serengeti Serena Lodge a good base in the centre of the park, and Klein's Camp for the Lobo area.

Ngorongoro Crater, Tanzania

(260 km²/100 sq. miles)

The eighth wonder of the world, and certainly worth stopping for two nights, not only for its unique geological features and stunning views, but also as home to some striking black-maned lions. You will be lucky to see cheetahs here, though you might catch sight of a leopard among the forests. The crater is an excellent place to view the endangered black rhino, with the ink-blue backdrop of the crater wall making the perfect scene-setter for wildlife photography. The birdlife is excellent, and the magnificent bull elephants with their long ivory tusks are always a favourite. If you are a keen photographer, or just want to get the best out of your stay, be sure to take a picnic breakfast as well as lunch. The misty morning atmosphere and chances of finding lions on the move make it well worth being out early.

Of the three lodges, Sopa Lodge provides the easiest access to the crater floor, while Ngorongoro Serena Lodge offers 75 rooms, all with crater views. If you just want luxury and fine food, it might almost be worth spending the day in your room, with a view to match, at the Ngorongoro Crater Lodge.

Selous Game Reserve, Tanzania

(43,000 km²/16,600 sq. miles)

Tanzania's southern wilderness is the place to take a walking safari in East Africa. This is 'old' Africa, wild bush country that harbours more than 100,000 buffaloes, nearly 60,000 elephants, the highest density of wild dogs anywhere in Africa and probably the largest single population of lions – with fewer tourists watching them. Even though the lions are not as numerous or as easy to see as in places such as the Mara and Serengeti, a visit to one of the tented camps along the Rufiji River is an ideal starting point for a walking safari. A boat trip along the river to watch giant crocodiles, large pods of hippos and elephants is a must, or you could simply take time out back at camp, to catch up with identifying some of the more than 440 species of birds.

Among the best of the camps are Sand Rivers Selous (particularly for those wanting to walk) and Selous Safari Camp (formerly known as Mbuyuni tented camp). A safari combining a visit to Selous and Ruaha National Park, and either Mahale Mountains or Gombe National Park to see chimpanzees, would be a great adventure away from the hustle and bustle of Tanzania's northern tourist circuit. But if it is easy wildlife watching that you want and your first fix of Africa, then Serengeti, Ngorongoro and Tarangire (1,360km²/525sq. miles), with its magnificent baobabs, large herds of elephants, excellent birdlife and a good chance of seeing lions and leopards, are hard to beat.

South Luangwa National Park, Zambia

(9,050 km²/3,500 sq miles)

Known locally as the Valley, this is where Norman Carr, one of Africa's most experienced safari guides, pioneered walking safaris. The Luangwa River dominates the park, providing a cooling and tranquil element. With the camps and lodges situated along the riverbanks, you can spend hours at a time watching the various animals coming to drink from the veranda of your tent – elephants, buffaloes, pukus, waterbucks, even lions and leopards. The best game-viewing is during winter (May–August) and the dry, hot months from September to November. Game concentrations tend to increase as the dry season progresses, but so too does the temperature. The rains (November–April) are excellent for birding, though most of the lodges and camps close at this time. The density of leopards is exceptional and lions are frequently seen. We visited in September, and during a night game drive – a highlight of any visit to Luangwa – saw one of the leopards that helped to make this area famous. Apart from looking for big cats, we spent many hours photographing elephants drinking and crossing the river, and enjoyed close-up views of the spectacular colonies of carmine bee-eaters that nest in the sandy banks.

There are a number of outfitters offering walking safaris, but Robin Pope Safaris is consistently recommended. The ideal time is probably late June to late September, for a five-day walk with a top guide, staying at mobile tented camps deep in the bush. Robin and Joe Pope also run three of the best permanent camps in the Valley: Nsefu, Tena Tena and Nkwali. A walking safari – even if only for a morning – is a must.

Kafue National Park, Zambia

(22,480 km²/8,680 sq. miles)

The second largest national park in Africa, comprising vast tracts of woodland and savanna bisected by the Kafue River. Surprisingly few people visit Kafue, considering that it is home to large herds of elephants, buffaloes, lions and leopards, and is renowned for its diversity of antelopes, with floodplains brimming with thousands of red lechwes and glimpses of magnificent sables and roans. There are cheetahs and wild dogs here, too, with large prides of lions hunting buffaloes on the Busanga Plain in the north. The animals tend to concentrate around water between July and October, with Busanga best between August and October.

There are only a handful of lodges, adding to the sense of wilderness. Among the best are Ntemwa and Busanga Bush camps, situated in the middle of the plains where lions are often seen; Lufupa Camp is well located for game drives and bush walks, with the chance of seeing leopard on night game drives.

Mana Pools National Park, Zimbabwe

(2,200 km²/850 sq. miles]

It is hard to think of Zimbabwe without planning a visit to the spectacular Victoria Falls and overnighting at the grand Victoria Falls Hotel. This is the place to take a canoe safari down the mighty Zambezi River, which forms the northern boundary of Mana Pools National Park. Hippos, crocodiles, elephants and buffaloes are all easily seen here. Mana is a likely spot to see lions, as is Matusadona National Park, which stretches up from the shores of Lake Kariba, and both offer the chance to walk or canoe, an exciting alternative to being driven around the African bush. John Stevens was one of the pioneers of canoe safaris and is one of Africa's top guides, specializing in walking and canoeing safaris, during which guests stay in mobile tented camps. Musangu and Muchichiri are two pleasant riverside lodges offering permanent accommodation, with Wilderness Safaris' Rukomechi and Chikwenya camps also highly recommended.

If you visit Lake Kariba, then Sanyati Lodge is among the best – you can relax, enjoy the lake and strike out on game drives, walks or fishing trips.

Moremi Game Reserve, Botswana

(3,900 km²/1,505 sq. miles)

The Okavango Delta is a huge oasis, an inland delta of wooded islands and papyrus swamps, whose crystal-clear waters disappear among the Kalahari sands. The delta rivals the Serengeti and Masai Mara as a wildlife spectacle, with excellent lion- and leopard-viewing, and a good chance of seeing cheetahs and wild dogs. The combination of water and wildlife is hard to beat, and the big-game viewing and birding opportunities are virtually limitless. The Moremi Reserve encompasses almost one third of the delta, and includes Chief's Island. The autumn/winter dry season (April–September) is best for wildlife viewing. There is an excellent chance of seeing wild dogs in June and July when they abandon their nomadic wandering for a few months and establish a den. Game-viewing reaches a peak during September and October, when animals congregate around permanent water, though temperatures can be high.

Many lodges close during the rainy season (December–March). There is a huge selection of camps and lodges to choose from, but among the best are Chief's Camp in the Mombo area, and Wilderness Safari's camps, Mombo and Little Mombo.

A visit to the Okavango Delta also offers the possibility of walking safaris, horseback safaris, even elephant-back safaris at Randall Moore's Abu's Camp, and a chance to walk with Doug Groves's elephants at Stanley's Camp. In the north, and bordering Namibia, Chobe National Park (11,700 km²/4,520 sq. miles) is home to large prides of lions and huge herds of buffaloes, and offers river trips to watch elephants crossing the Chobe River. In the west of the park, the Linyanti Marsh and Savuti areas are famous for their lion-viewing, though it can be very seasonal. Chobe is a good place to visit en route to Victoria Falls, stopping over at Chobe Chilwero Lodge.

Okonjima and the Africat Foundation, Namibia

(135 km²/52 sq. miles)

Namibia is home to more cheetahs than any other African country, with perhaps 3,000 of these elegant cats. But 95 per cent are found on private ranchland, where they often run into conflict with ranchers. Lise Hanssen and her team at the Africat Foundation have dedicated themselves to working with ranchers to lessen conflict with predators, removing animals that are trapped and might otherwise be shot or poisoned. They work mainly with cheetahs and leopards, but also with servals, caracals and the occasional lion, supporting a number of research and education projects.

The Hanssens have turned the family home at Okonjima ranch into comfortable guest accommodation, providing visitors with the chance to visit the Africat Foundation and meet some of the cheetahs. Photographers will find plenty of interest here, and a visit to the leopard blind in the evening is an experience not to be missed. Lise has also helped to found the Predator Conservation Trust (website details on p.123).

The Cheetah Conservation Fund (CCF), Otjiwarongo, Namibia

CCF was the brainchild of Laurie Marker and Daniel Kraus, and is dedicated to the long-term survival of the cheetah through research and education. Laurie and her team are at the hub of cheetah conservation and, like the Africat Foundation, work closely with ranchers, providing a home for orphaned cheetahs trapped on ranchland. CCF has pioneered the use of guard dogs to help farmers reduce stock losses to predators, and has placed well over 160 Anatolian Shepherd dogs with farmers. Where possible wild-caught adult cheetahs are relocated. The excellent Visitor Education Centre at CCF is open to the public.

To see wild cheetahs in Namibia, the best option is to visit Etosha National Park (22,270 km²/8,600 sq. miles). Natural springs and artificial waterholes (such as the Okaukuejo waterhole) dotted along the southern edge of the stark Etosha Pan at the heart of the park provide the focal point for game-viewing, attracting large numbers of animals, such as wildebeest, zebras, springboks, gemsboks and elands. Though all three big cats are found here, there is no guarantee that you will see them. If big cats are the priority and time is short then perhaps this is not the place for you; otherwise it is memorable.

Namib-Naukluft Park, Namibia

(49,754 km²/19,210 sq. miles)

This enormous wilderness stretches from Luderitz in the south to Swakopmund in the north. Not the place to see big cats, but as a safari destination it is a world apart, a vast moonscape with towering dunes, which are transformed when the summer rains come – if they come – in December to February. The extraordinary creeping welwitschia plants are endemic to the Namib and can live for more than 2,000 years. Sossusvlei Mountain Lodge in the adjoining Namib Rand Nature Reserve, and Wilderness Sossusvlei Camp are among the best, offering a variety of activities including day trips to the towering dunes of Sossusvlei. There is even a star-gazing safari with the help of a giant telescope at Mountain Lodge – not to be missed.

Kruger National Park, South Africa

(19,480 km²/7,520 sq. miles)

This is South Africa's premier national park, with more mammal and bird species than any other park in the country. All of the 'big five' can be found here – lions, leopards, buffaloes, rhinos and elephants – as well as cheetahs and wild dogs, with the southern area of the park offering the greatest variety of landscape and the best game-viewing. The one big limitation has always been that you are confined to tarmac roads. However, the parks authorities have recently put out to tender a number of private concessions, where off-road driving and walking safaris from small camps and lodges will add a whole new dimension to a safari in Kruger. Game-viewing is best during winter (May–October), when animals concentrate at water sources. The rainy season is from October to March.

Sabi Sands Game Reserve, South Africa (including Londolozi and Mala Mala)

(650 km²/250 sq. miles)

There are a number of private game reserves clustered along the western boundary of the Kruger that are no longer separated from it by fencing. These offer excellent opportunities for big cat enthusiasts, and are particularly worth a visit if your passion is leopards. The most famous is Londolozi (130km²/50sq. miles), which has been transformed by John and Dave Varty since they took over the lodge in the early 1970s and restored the area to its former glory. Also well worth a visit is Mala Mala – both of these virtually guarantee leopard sightings. When we visited Londolozi we saw three different leopards on five separate occasions, as well as three magnificent male lions and plenty of cubs, white rhinos, elephants and two glorious kudu bulls.

Night game drives are a feature at all the lodges, and a good way to see leopards, though the rangers work hard to track them down during daytime as well, with off-the-road driving the norm. Cheetahs and wild dogs are not uncommonly seen. Ngala, Sabi Sabi, Singita and Idube lodges are all recommended.

Phinda Resource Reserve, South Africa

(180 km²/70 sq. miles)

Lions and cheetahs have been introduced to this private game reserve, and it is certainly a good place to photograph them – particularly cheetahs, which are almost guaranteed. But getting a clear view of them usually depends on being able to drive off-road, and this is restricted after annual burning, so be sure to check first. All the 'big five' are here, and leopards are quite often seen. Winter (May–October) is the dry season and the best time for clear sightings. Accommodation is in four luxury lodges. Phinda offers a number of extensions. You can opt to walk in search of black rhino in the adjacent Mkuzi Game Reserve, dive on the east coast coral reefs or fly over Greater St Lucia Wetland Park.

Further Information:

Websites

African National Parks
www.newafrica.com/nationalparks/
Africat
www.africat.org/
Cheetah Conservation Fund
www.cheetah.org
Big Cats Online
dialspace.dial.pipex.com/agarman/bco/ver4.htm
Big Cat Research
www.bigcats.com
IUCN Cat Specialist Group
lynx.uio.no/catfolk
The Lion Research Centre
(lions of the Serengeti and Ngorongoro Crater)
www.lionresearch.org
Friends of Conservation
(conservation body involved in the Mara)
www.foc-uk.com
Predator Conservation Trust
lise@predatortrust.org
Campfire Conservation Limited
(community conservation initiatives in Kenya)
campfire@africaonline.co.ke

Tour Operators

Abercrombie and Kent (East and southern Africa)
http://www.abercrombiekent.co.uk
Afro Ventures (East and southern Africa)
http://www.afroventures.com
Conservation Corporation Africa
(East and southern Africa)
http://www.ccafrica.com
East African Wildlife Safaris (Kenya)
mailto:eaws@kenyaweb.com
Gibb's Farm Safaris (Tanzania)
mailto:ndutugibbs@nabari.co.tz
John Stevens Safaris
(Zimbabwe canoe/walking safaris)
mailto:bushlife@hare.iafrica.com
Okavango Tours and Safaris (Botswana)
http://www.okavango.com
Richard Bonham Safaris
(Tanzania – Selous specialist)
mailto:Bonham.Luke@swiftkenya.com
Robin Pope Safaris
(Zambia – Luangwa Valley specialist)
mailto:popesaf@zamnet.zm
Wilderness Safaris (southern Africa specialists)
mailto:outposts@usa.net
Governor's Camp
(Kenya/Masai Mara tented camps)
mailto:info@governorscamp.com
Worldwide Journeys and Expeditions
(African safari specialists)
www.worldwidejourneys.co.uk

Bibliography

It would have been impossible to write this book without leaning heavily on the work of other authors. We're particularly grateful to Dr Luke Hunter, author of *Cheetah*, who was incredibly generous with his time, providing us with invaluable information on Africa's big cats, as well as many contacts among predator researchers working in southern Africa. Here in Nairobi, Judith Rudnai kindly shared her excellent library of books and articles with us. Gus Mills at Kruger Park in South Africa was a fund of knowledge on Africa's large predators and provided copies of scientific articles. In Namibia, Lise Hanssen and the AfriCat Foundation, and Laurie Marker at the Cheetah Conservation Fund were generous with their time and information, and amazingly hospitable, as were the rest of the Hanssen family at Okonjima. Our Nairobi neighbours, Esmond Bradley-Martin and his wife Chryssee, were a mine of information on matters relating to wildlife conservation, and generously allowed us access to back issues of *Cat News*, the newsletter of the Species Survival Commission (IUCN), which I would highly recommend to anyone with a passion for the world's wild cats. Tim Caro's book *Cheetahs of the Serengeti Plains* is a goldmine of information on these predators, and David Burney's MSc thesis on the Mara cheetahs is an inspirational model for good field work. Finally, for an all-encompassing portrait of the lives of the world's 36 species of cats, you need look no further than *Wild Cats of the World* by Mel and Fiona Sunquist.

We are only too well aware of the dangers of interpreting the work of others, particularly when trying to present information gleaned from scientific papers. Accordingly, while we are indebted to the following authors, they remain blameless for any inaccuracies in our text, and we apologize for the inevitable simplifications.

Adamson, J. *The Spotted Sphinx*. Collins: London 1969
Ames, E. *A glimpse of Eden*. Collins: London 1968
Ammann, K. 'A response to the "Survival of the swiftest"'. *Swara*, Vol 16, No.2. 1993
Ammann, K. & Amman, K. *Cheetah*. Camerapix: Nairobi 1984
Bailey, T. N. *The African Leopard: ecology and behaviour of a solitary felid*. Columbia University Press: New York 1993
Bothma, J du P. & Walker, C. *Larger Carnivores of the African Savannas*. J. L. van Schaik: Pretoria 1999
Bottriell, L. G. *King Cheetah: the story of the quest*. E. J. Brill: Leiden 1987
Boy, G. 'The Count Continues'. *Swara*, Vol 26, No.1 2003
—— 'Tale of the Ten Cubs'. *Safari*, August/September 1998
Burney, D. A. 'The effects of human activities on cheetah (*Acinonyx jubatus*) in the Mara region of Kenya'. MSc thesis, University of Nairobi 1980
Burney, D. A., & Burney, L. 'Cheetah and Man'. *Swara*, Vol 2, No 2. 1979
Caro, T. *Cheetahs of the Serengeti Plains: group living in an asocial species*. University of Chicago Press: Chicago & London 1994
Caro, T & Laurenson, K. 'The Serengeti Cheetah Project'. *Swara*, Vol 12, No 2. 1989
Cavanaugh, J. Cheetahs of Nairobi National Park (1993–1998), private correspondence 1998
Clark, A & Lubbe, T. 'Namibia – Last outpost for the cheetah'. *African Wildlife*, 49/5:13–4 (August 1995)
Conniff, R. 'Cheetahs: Ghosts of the Grasslands'. *National Geographic*, Vol.196, No.6. 1999
Drummond, D. 'Operation Cheetah'. *Swara* Vol 12, No 3. 1989
Eaton, R. L. *The Cheetah: the biology, ecology, and behaviour of an endangered species*. Van Nostrand Reinhold: New York 1974
Estes, R. D. *The Behavior Guide to African Mammals: including hoofed mammals, carnivores, primates*. University of California Press: Oxford 1991
Frame, G. W. & Frame, L. H. 'Serengeti Cheetahs'. *Swara*, Vol 16, No 5. 1993.
—— *Swift and Enduring*. Elsevier–Dutton: New York 1981
Grzimek, B, & Grzimek, M. *Serengeti Shall Not Die*. Hamish Hamilton: London 1960.
Hall-Martin, A, & Bosman, P. *Cats of Africa*. Swan Hill Press, an imprint of Airlife Publishing: London 1997
Hamman, D, & Hunter, L. T. B. *Cheetah*. Struik 2003
Holmes, M. 'Cheetah Hunting in the Kalahari'. *African Wildlife* Vol 35, No 6 1981
Hunter, L. T. B. *Cheetahs*. Colin Baxter Photography: Granton-on-Spey 2000
—— 'Fighting Tooth and Claw: the future of Africa's magnificent cats.' *Africa Geographic*. Vol. 9 (5): 46-56 2001
Hunter, L.T.B. & Skinner, J. D. 'Do male cheetahs *Acinonyx jubatus* commit infanticide?' *Trans. Roy. Soc. S. Afr.* 58 (1) pages 79-82 2003
Jackman, B.J. 'Cat Watching, Africa: lions, leopards and cheetahs: where to see them'. *BBC Wildlife*, Vol.19, No.2 2001
Jackman, B. J., & Scott, J. P. *The Marsh Lions*. Elm Tree Books: London 1982
—— *The Big Cat Diary*. BBC Books: London 1996
Kingdon, J. *East African Mammals: an atlas of evolution in Africa*. Vol.3, part A (Carnivores), Academic Press: London 1977.
Laurenson, M. K. 'Reproductive Strategies in Wild Female Cheetahs. PhD dissertation, University of Cambridge 1992

Macdonald, D. *The Velvet Claw: a natural history of the carnivores*. BBC Books: London 1992

Marker, L., Kraus, D., Barnett, D., & Hurlbut, S. *Cheetah Survival on Namibian Farmlands*. Cheetah Conservation Fund (CCF) 1996

Marker-Kraus, L., & Kraus, D. 'The History of Cheetahs in Namibia'. *Swara* Vol 16 No 5 1993

McLaughlin, R.T. 'Aspects of the Biology of the Cheetah (*Acinonyx jubatus*, Schreber) in Nairobi National Park'. MSc thesis, University of Nairobi 1970

Mills, G., & Harvey, M. *African Predators*. Struik: South Africa 2001

Morsbach, D. 'The Behavioural Ecology and Movement of Cheetahs on Farmland in Southwest Africa/Namibia'. Annual reports, Department of Agriculture & Nature Conservation, Directorate of Nature Conservation & Recreational Resorts, Government of Namibia, Windhoek 1984/86

Moss, C. *Portraits in the Wild: animal behaviour in East Africa*. Elm Tree Books: London 1989.

Myers, N. *The Long African Day*, Macmillan: New York 1972

—— 'Status of the Leopard and Cheetah in Africa' in *The World's Cats*, Vol.3(1), ed. R. L. Eaton, 48-59. Carnivore Research Institute, University of Washington, Seattle 1976

Neff, N.A. *The Big Cats: the paintings of Guy Coheleach*. Harry N. Abrams: New York 1982.

Nowell, K., & Jackson, P. *Wild Cats: status survey and conservation action plan*, IUCN/SSC Cat Specialist Group, IUCN: Gland, Switzerland 1996

Schaller, G.B. *The Serengeti Lion: a study of predator-prey relations*. University of Chicago Press: Chicago 1972

—— *Serengeti: a kingdom of predators*. Collins: London 1973

Schroeder-MacNaughton, J. 'Survival of the Swiftest', *Swara*, Vol 15, No.3 1992

Scott, J.P. *The Leopard's Tale*. Elm Tree Books: London 1985

—— *The Great Migration*. Elm Tree Books: London 1988

—— *Painted Wolves: wild dogs of the Serengeti–Mara*. Hamish Hamilton: London 1991

—— *Kingdom of Lions*. Kyle Cathie: London 1992

—— *Dawn to Dusk: a safari through Africa's wild places*. BBC Books in association with Kyle Cathie: London 1996

—— *Jonathan Scott's Safari Guide to East African Animals* (revised & updated by Angela Scott). Kensta: Nairobi 1997

—— *Jonathan Scott's Safari Guide to East African Birds* (revised & updated by Angela Scott). Kensta: Nairobi 1997

Scott, J. P., & Scott, A. 'Death on the Rocks (infanticide in leopards)'. *BBC Wildlife*, Vol.16 No.4 April 1998

—— *Mara-Serengeti: a photographer's paradise*.

Fountain Press, London 2000.

—— *Big Cat Diary: Lion*. HarperCollins: London 2002

—— *Big Cat Diary*: Leopard. HarperCollins: London 2003

Seidensticker, J., & Lumpkin, S., (eds). *Great Cats: majestic creatures of the wild*. Merehurst: London 1991

Shales, M. *African Safari*. Discovery Communications: 2000

Sinclair, A. R. E., & Norton-Griffiths, M., (eds.). *Serengeti: dynamics of an ecosystem*. University of Chicago Press: Chicago 1979

Sinclair, A. R. E., & Arcese, P., (eds.). *Serengeti II: dynamics, management, and conservation of an ecosystem*. University of Chicago Press: Chicago 1995

Sunquist, M, & Sunquist, F. *Wild Cats of the World*. University of Chicago Press: Chicago & London 2002

Turner, A., & Anton, M. *The Big Cats and their Fossil Relatives: an illustrated guide to their evolution and natural history*. Columbia University Press: New York 1997.

Turner, M. *My Serengeti Years: the memoirs of an African game warden*. ed. Jackman, B. Elm Tree Books: London 1987

van Lawick, H. *Savage Paradise*. Collins: London 1977

Whitfield, P. *The Hunters*. Hamlyn: London 1978

Wrogemann, N. *Cheetah under the Sun*. McGraw-Hill: Johannesburg 1975

Wykstra, M. 'Outside Chance'. *Swara*, Vol 25, No.2 2002

—— (ed). 'Workshop on cheetah conservation in Kenya', sponsored by Cheetah Conservation Fund & African Wildlife Foundation, 30–31 July 2003

Acknowledgements

We have received such generous support from so many individuals and companies that it is possible to mention only a few of them here.

We would like to thank the governments of Kenya and Tanzania for allowing us to live and work in the Serengeti–Mara, and to acknowledge the assistance of Tanzania National Parks, and both the Narok and Trans Mara County Councils, who administer the Masai Mara National Game Reserve. Over the years Senior Wardens John Naiguran, Simon Makallah, Michael Koikai, Stephen Minis and James Sindiyo in the Mara, and David Babu and Bernard Maregesi in the Serengeti have all been helpful and supportive of our projects, as have Brian Heath and Jonny Baxendale of the Mara Conservancy that manages the Mara Triangle.

Thanks to everyone involved in *Big Cat Diary* (*BCD*), both here in Kenya and at the Natural History Unit (NHU) in Bristol. To 'field commander' Keith Scholey, and series producer Fiona Pitcher, for supporting the idea of this series of books, and to Keith and his wife Liz, Robin and Elin Hellier, and Mandy Knight and Andy Chastney for welcoming us into their homes when we visit the NHU. The success of *BCD* relies on people working together, and as much as anyone, Mandy Knight, production manager of *BCD* (series 1 to 4) and Jenni Collie epitomize the combination of professionalism and big-heartedness which makes working on *BCD* such a privilege and pleasure.

Rosamund Kidmund-Cox, former editor of *BBC Wildlife* magazine, has been a great friend and loyal supporter of our work over the years, and helped us to believe that there was room for yet more books on Africa's big cats. We wish her well in her new ventures.

Myles Archibald at HarperCollins commissioned this series of three titles featuring Africa's big cats, beginning with *Lion* and *Leopard*. Myles' enthusiasm for the project helped to spur us on. Helen Brocklehurst, our editor at HarperCollins, has been a pleasure to work with, full of optimism and new ideas, and Liz Sephton, our designer, managed to add her own brand of creative flare in record time.

Caroline Taggart has edited all but one of our books, but even someone as unflappable as Caroline realized that once again she was going to have to call on all her considerable editing skills – and an uncanny ability to make her authors feel that anything is possible – if we were to complete the cheetah book on time. That we did says much for Caroline's many talents. Thank you again.

Jonathan Pegg, our literary agent at Curtis Brown, has been wonderfully supportive and continues to manage our affairs with great charm and professionalism.

Our wildlife photographs are held by three picture libraries: NHPA, ImageState and Getty Images. Tim Harris and his team at NHPA generously allowed us to rifle the cheetah files at short notice for this book, as did Diana Leppard at ImageState.

Both Angie and I have family living overseas who has been an unfailing source of help and encouragement. Now that my sister Caroline has moved from England to sunny Portugal, my brother Clive and his wife Judith have kindly inherited the boxes of books and slides that used to live at Caroline's house in Inkpen. Angie's mother Joy still lives in England but sadly hasn't enjoyed the best of health recently, and her brother David and wife Mishi now live in France. We miss them all.

Pam Savage and Michael Skinner have taken us under their wing these past few years, offering advice and reassurance when needed, and allowing us the freedom of their home in London. It is difficult to know how to thank friends like that adequately. Cissy and David Walker have been equally forthcoming with their generosity and good fellowship, and this book is dedicated to them. Frank and Dolcie Howitt continue to be the best of neighbours to us here in Nairobi, and are very dear friends.

Many other people have provided us with a second home during our visits to England over the years, particularly Pippa and Ian Stewart-Hunter, Paul and Donna Goldstein, Ken and Lois Kuhle, and Martin and Avril Freeth in London; Brian and Annabelle Jackman in Dorset; Dr Michael and Sue Budden in Buckinghamshire; and Charles and Lindsay Dewhurst in West Sussex – all wonderful hosts and friends who put up with our comings and goings with admirable tolerance.

We have shared some wonderful times with our good friends Neil and Joyce Silverman in Africa, Antarctica and at their beautiful home in Florida. They have helped us in many ways over the years, and are always there when we need them.

Carole Wyman has been a loyal and generous friend to Angie since they met in Kenya many years ago, and is godmother to our son David. Carol is an individual of rare qualities, and our only regret is that we see so little of her and her husband Khama.

Jock Anderson of East African Wildlife Safaris continues to be a great friend to our family. He gave me the chance to live at Mara River Camp 28 years ago, a gift of such magnitude that I shall never forget his role in making it possible. Stephen Masika, Jock's office messenger, still keeps track of correspondence and renews licences for us with unfailing efficiency.

Aris, Justin and Dominic Grammaticus have been generous in allowing us to base ourselves at Governor's Camp, and George Murray is the most marvelous host at Little Governor's Camp in the Mara Triangle. Patrick Reynolds has made a reputation for himself as a top-class walking-safari guide at Il Murran, and always makes us welcome at this most luxurious among the Governor's family of camps. Patrick Beresford and his staff at Governor's Workshop somehow managed to keep us on the road, regardless of the damage we inflicted on our Toyota Landcruiser, and all with a smile. You are simply the best, Patrick.

Finally, we would like to acknowledge the invaluable help of Shigeru Ito of Toyota East Africa, Canon Camera Division (UK), Hazel Smith at Kenya Airways (UK), Anna Nzomo at Air Kenya, Mehmood and Shaun Quraishy at Spectrum Colour Lab (Nairobi), Pankaj Patel of Fuji Kenya, Jan Mohamed of Serena Hotels, David Leung, the Canon Camera specialist at Goodmayes Road, Ilford (UK), and Christine Percy at Swarovski Optic (UK), all of whom have made life in the bush tenable through their ongoing support.

We are truly fortunate in being able to follow our passion as a career. But the joy that this brings pales alongside the inspiration and love we derive from our children Alia and David. May their lives be equally blessed.

Index

Page numbers in *italic* refer to illustrations